DIE GOUGES AND SCRATCHES
PEACE DOLLAR ATTRIBUTION GUIDE

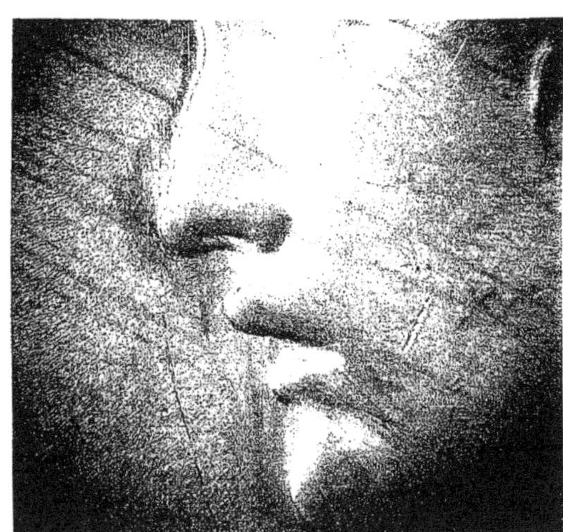

1923 D VAM 1BK3 Die Gouges/Scratches Face

1924 P VAM 1A Feed Fingers Gouge D

October 2013

1922 P VAM 1A Die Edge Gouge Rays

1923 P VAM 1AC1 X Die Scratches

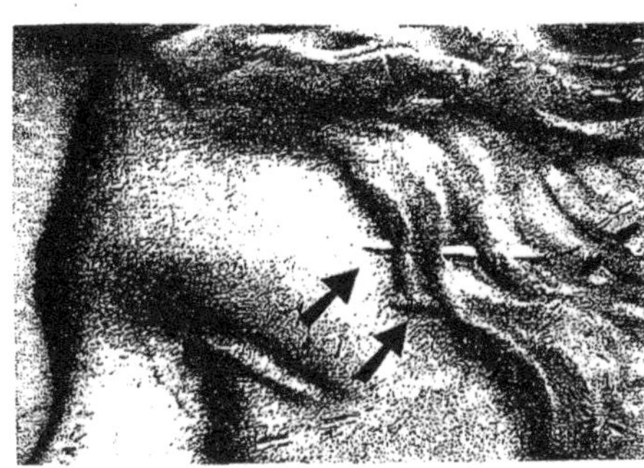

1922 P VAM 2N Double Die Edge Gouges

Published by

Rare Coin Investments (RCI)
P.O. Box C
Ironia, NJ 07845

Authors: Leroy C. Van Allen
Edited by: Michael S. Fey, Ph.D.

ISBN-13 number: 979-8-9919648-8-3

Printed in the United States

TABLE OF CONTENTS

DIE GOUGES AND SCRATCHES ON PEACE DOLLARS ATTRIBUTION GUIDE

INTRODUCTION

The many die gouges and scratches that have been reported over the years on both the obverse and reverse dies of Peace dollars is treated in this attribution guide. To date, there have been reported **270** die gouges and scratches. This guide **identifies** and **explores** some of the **causes** of the die gouges and scratches that include **feed fingers**, **die edges** and **two dies jousted together**. There are also many gouges and scratches of peculiar shapes and sizes that have no ready explanation as of yet.

Most of the die gouges and scratches on Peace dollars were reported **from 1998 onwards**. This was because of fewer Peace dollar collectors than those of Morgan dollar die varieties before that time. But the gain in popularity of Peace dollars in the past fifteen years has resulted in an **explosion** of reported die varieties for this series.

The so-called **VAM book** was named after the authors, *Comprehensive Catalog & Encyclopedia of Morgan And Peace Dollars* by Leroy C.. Van Allen & A. George Mallis, third edition, 1992, and WorldWide Ventures reprint of third edition, 1998. It only had **three** listed and pictured die gouges of one each for 1922 P, 1923 P and 1924 P. Recent books on Peace dollar die varieties include:

- *The Official Guide To The Top 50 Peace Dollar Varieties* by Jeff Oxman and Dr. David Close, 2002 (Includes **five** die gouges varieties)
- *A Guide Book of Peace Dollars* by Roger W. Burdette with Barry Lovvorn, Whitman Pub., 2008 (Includes **seven** die gouges varieties)
- *Wonders of Peace Dollars* by Leroy Van Allen, 2012 (Includes **all reported die gouges varieties** of over **200** thru May 2012)
- *The Elite 30 Peace Dollar VAMs* by Dr. David Close and C. Ash Harrison, 2013 (Includes **three** die gouges varieties)

Collectors are invited to examine these interesting coins and assemble collections of this special category of die varieties. There are some truly **amazing** and **different** die gouges that can be found as detailed in this guide. **Gouges** are **wide and thick bars** and **scratches** are **thin raised lines** on coins. They range greatly in size and length and only those **readily visible to the naked eye** are listed as die varieties. Fine polishing lines and areas that not visible to the naked eye aren't listed but can sometimes be useful as die markers. They are **not included** in this guide.

Some objectives of this guide are to make collectors aware of the **large number** of die gouge varieties, the **types** and their **causes** and to serve as a **reference catalogue**. Recognition is given to collectors who specifically reported the die gouges and scratches varieties. The type of die gouges and scratches are briefly described and illustrated followed by detailed discussion, explanation and photographs of their various causes. Another chapter investigates the die rim edge notch dimensions and possible impacts on the die face. A chapter of the author's Top 30 die gouges is provided, but readers are invited to **consider their own favorite choices**. Descriptive listings of **all reported die gouges to date** are presented followed by their photographs in Appendices A– D.

The author can be contacted about possible unlisted die gouges and scratches die varieties at:

Leroy Van Allen
P.O. Box 196
Sidney, OH 45365
or by e-mail at vams@woh.rr.com

REPORTING OF GOUGES AND SCRATCHES DIE VARIETIES

This chapter lists the current **VAM numbers** for the **270** various types of die variety gouges and scratches that have been reported for the Peace dollars. It includes the **collector** who reported each die gouge variety and the **date reported**. This is shown in the following listing, **Die Gouges Discoverers Hall Of Fame**. In some cases it was a revision of an existing VAM number listed for other reasons than a die gouge, such as a doubled die, die break or die file lines. Only the collector who reported the die gouge is mentioned in the list of discoverers and not any other collector who reported other types of die varieties.

There have been early listings of errors and die varieties without photographs in the 1950's and early 1960's. But any of these that were mentioned as die gouges were not examined and photographed by the author at that time. Only when the author began listing and photographing die varieties from 1965 onwards were Van Allen numbers assigned and later in the 1971 and subsequent editions of the Van Allen and Mallis VAM books were VAM numbers assigned.

The **first reported** die gouge on a Peace dollar die that became an **assigned VAM number** was the strong vertical die gouge from the D in GOD of **VAM 1A** for the **1924 P**. It was reported by Bill Fivaz in January 1974 without a specific cause. It was later determined to be caused by mal-functioning feed fingers.

The next listed vertical die gouge by feed fingers on the lower obverse was the **1923 P VAM 1F** reported by Jon Steinberg in July 1982. An early beveled field from feed fingers was reported by Robert Varoe in March 2006 for the **1923 P VAM 1Z.** For the thin die gouges in the obverse rays from the reverse die edge, the first reported was the **1922 P VAM 2F** by Leroy Van Allen in February 1983 without mention of a cause. Double die edge gouges on the obverse have only recently been recognized in 2013 as such. But a number have been listed as die gouges with two or several closely spaced parallel lines with no cause given at the time, such as the **1922 P VAM 1E/2L** reported by David Close in January 2000 and **1922 P VAM 2N** reported by Bill Van Note in February 2000.

Fine line die gouges on reverse dies that were possibly caused by die edges have also only been recognized in 2013. But the early reporting of the die gouges on the reverse was the **1923 D VAM 1G** reported by David Close in May 2001 and the **1923 P VAM 1Q** reported by Jeff Oxman in October 2001. Some early unexplained, without a specific cause, die gouges were reported by Jeff Oxman in April 1999 for the **1923 VAM 1I,** the **1922 S VAM 2A** by Bill Van Note in December 1999 and the **1923 D VAM 1A** by David Close in December 1999.

By far, **David Close** has reported the **greatest number of die variety gouges** on Peace dollars from late 1999 onwards. **Jeff Oxman** and **Larry Briggs** reported quite a few die gouges during the late 1990s and early 2000s. Various collectors have reported die gouges from 2000 onwards as collector interest in Peace dollar die varieties has greatly increased.

Leroy Van Allen September 2013

DIE GOUGES DISCOVERERS HALL OF FAME

VAM	Discoverer	Date
1921 Peace		
1B	David Close	May 02
1E	" "	Sep 04
1E2	" "	June 06
1J	William Bland	June 06
1K	David Close	Aug 06
1T	Kevin Frank	Dec 06
1X	Bill Toland	Sep 11
1922 P		
1A/39	Jeff Oxman	Apr 99
1B	David Close`	Nov 99
1C/40	" "	Jan 00
1D	" "	Jan 00
1E/2L	" "	Jan 00
1H	Leroy Van Allen	Dec 00
1J	Brent Fogelberg	Nov 02
1M	David Close	Mar 07
1P	" "	Nov 07
1Q	" "	Sep 08
1S	Jason Henrichsen	Apr 10
1U	David Close	Jan 12
1X	Jason Henrichsen	Oct 12
2Erevise	Herb Zepke	Jan 99
2F	Leroy Van Allen	Feb 83
2Frevise	Ben Wengel	Sep 09
2H	Jeff Oxman	Feb 98
2J	" "	Apr 99
2K	David Close	Nov 99
2M	" "	Jan 00
2N	Bill Van Note	Feb 00
2O	David Close	Apr 00
2P1	David Close	Apr 00
2P2	Jason Henrichsen	Apr 10
2Q	David Close	Sep 00
2R	" "	Sep 00
2S	" "	Dec 00
2W	" "	Nov 02
2Y	" "	Jan 03
2Z	" "	Jan 03
2AC	" "	Sep 03
2AD	" "	May 04
2AE	Larry Briggs	May 04
2AI	David Close	Sep 04
2AK	" "	Jan 05
2AL	" "	Jan 05
2AM	" "	Feb 05
2AS/AG	Laurence Galbraith	May 05
2AU	David Close	May 05

2AW David Close July 05
2AX Laurence Galbraith Aug 05
2BJ Mark Kleiman Aug 06
2BL James Cerny Aug 06
2BM Eric Justice Aug 06
2BO John Vernieri Oct 06
2BP James Cerny Aug 06
2BQ David Close Nov 06
2BV Michael Ash Apr 07
2BW David Close May 07
2BZ Pat Signore Mar 08
2CB Michael Ash Aug 08
2CCrevise John Coxe Dec 09
2CG Jason Henrichsen Mar 09
2CH Ben Wengel June 09
2CN Ben Wengel Sep 09
2CQ James Cerny Mar 10
2CR David Close May 10
2CU Ben Wengel Aug 10
2CW Larry Briggs Sep 10
2CX James Cerny Jan 11
2DD David Close Jan 12
2DE " " Jan 12
2DG Jason Henrichsen Feb 12
2DH John Baumgart Feb 12
2DM David Close June 12
2DQ Jason Henrichsen Sep 12
3revise Michael Ash Nov 12
5-2 Jeff Oxman Aug 11
5A1 Christian Merlo Aug 09
5C Jeff Oxman Aug 11
18 Michael Ash Sep 06
22A Ben Wengel Apr 10
25B Chuck Emery Jan 11
29A Ben Wengel Feb 09
31A William Bland Oct 06
34A Pat Mullen Mar 10
40/2C David Close Jan 00
54A David Close Sep 08

1922 D

1F Larry Briggs Aug 02
1P David Close Sep 04
1AA John Bradley Feb 10
2W David Close Sep 03
2BJ Jason Henrichsen June 12
2BO Jason Henrichsen Dec 12
5 Jeff Oxman Sep 99
7 Jeff Oxman Oct 11
8revise Norman Salter Dec 08
13B John Vernieri Feb 08

1922 S

1A Herb Zepke Mar 00
1AD David Close June 12
2A Bill Van Note Dec 99
2C1 David Close Aug 01
2D/2J1 " " Nov 02
2E " " Dec 04
2I Laurence Galbraith Apr 05
2K David Close July 05
2M " " Nov 05
2N1/2AG " " Jan 06
2U " " July 09
2Z " " Nov 10
2AB " " Feb 11
2AI " " June 12
5A " " Sep 03

1923 P

1Crevise John Vernieri May 07
1F Jon Steinberg July 82
1G Jeff Oxman Feb 98
1I " " Apr 99
1J " " Oct 99
1K David Close Nov 99
1L Jeff Oxman Nov 99
1M David Close Dec 99
1N " " Feb 00
1P " " Dec 00
1Q Jeff Oxman Oct 01
1R " " Oct 01
1T Larry Briggs July 02
1U David Close Nov 02
1X " " Sep 03
1Z George Powell Apr 04
1AB1 Michael Ash Sep 06
1AC1 David Close May 04
1AD " " May 04
1AG Laurence Galbraith Apr 05
1AI " " May 05
1AJ David Close July 05
1AK Laurence Galbraith July 05
1AM Norman Salter Oct 05
1AO Norman Salter Jan 06
1AS David Close June 06
1BA John Vernieri Apr 07
1BC Christian Merlo Feb 08
1BE Ralph Wilson Feb 08
1BF David Close June 08
1BG John Roberts Aug 08
1BH Richard Carlson Jan 09
1BI Jason Henrichsen Feb 09
1BL Jason Henrichsen July 09
1BM Benjamin Underwood Sep 09
1BO Ben Wengel June 10
1BR John Vernieri Jan 11
1BS " " Feb 11
1BT " " Feb 11
1BY David Close June 12
1CB " " Nov 12
1CC " " Mar 13
1CF " " July 13
1CH Leroy Van Allen July 13
4A Pat Signore Mar 08
7A Rob Latour May 11
11revise John Vernieri Feb 07

1923 D

1A David Close Dec 99
1D1 " " Apr 00
1G " " May 01
1V Larry Briggs Aug 03
1AG Brian Raines Sep 04
1AN David Close July 05
1AO1 David Borofski Feb 06
1AX1 Brian Raines June 06
1BI James Cerny Dec 09
1BK1 David Close Jan 10
1BK2 David Close Feb 11
1BK3 Brian Raines Feb 11
1BS Jason Henrichsen June 10
1CB Brian Raines Mar 11
1CC James Cerny Apr 11
1CE John Baumgart Sep 11
1CF David Close June 12

1923 S

1H Jim Hart Nov 02
1V David Close May 05
1AD3 " " Feb 11
1AO " " Nov 06
1AQ1 John Vernieri Jan 07
1AZrevise James Cerny Mar 10
1BI James Cerny Mar 10
1BK James Cerny Mar 10
1BW David Close Feb 11
1BX Paul Olson May 11
1CP David Close Mar 13
1CR Larry Briggs Feb 13

1924 P

1A1 Bill Fivaz Jan 74
1E David Close Sep 00
1F Eric Justice June 01
1J Larry Briggs July 02
1K1 Larry Briggs Aug 02
1L David Close Nov 02
1M " " Sep 03
1N " " May 04
1O Eric Justice Nov 04
1S David Close Feb 05
1U David Close July 05
1Y Laurence Galbraith Dec 05
1Z David Close Jan 06
1AD David Close June 06
1AI John Vernieri Jan 07
1AJ John Vernieri Feb 07
1AL David Close Nov 07
1AP Pat Mullen Jan 10
1AR Felix Gonzales Apr 10
1AS James Cerny May 10
1AT Pat Mullen May 10
1AU David Close May 10
1AV Bill Latour June 10
1AY Larry Briggs Oct 10
1BE David Close Sep 11
1BT Larry Briggs Feb 13
8Brevise Jason Henrichsen Feb 10

1924 S

1C David Close June 06
1H Larry Briggs Sep 10
1J Tim Hargis Feb 11
1L Jason Henrichsen Mar 13
3revise Steve Bandovich Sep 10

1925 P

1A Jeff Oxman Apr 99
1B Jim Hart July 03
1D David Close Sep 03
1E Eric Justice Nov 04
1F Eric Justice Dec 04
1P David Close June 06
1Q " " Aug 06
1S " " Nov 06
1AA " " May 10
1AB John Vernieri June 10
1AD Paul Olson Dec 10
1AF James Cerny Feb 11
1AG David Close Sep 11
1AI John Baumgart Dec 11
1AM Ray Castro Mar 13
1AN Leroy Van Allen July 13
2A Pat Mullen Nov 09
9A David Close Feb 05
11A Richard Verde May 05
17A John Coxe Apr 08
18A Jason Henrichsen Feb 12

1925 S

1A1 Benjamin Underwood Jan 09
1A2 David Close Sep 00
1C Laurence Galbraith May 05
1F Benjamin Underwood Jan 09

1926 P

1C1	Norman Salter	Oct 05
3A	Laurence Galbraith	June 07
4A	John Ginder	Mar 07

1926 D

1C	Jason Henrichsen	Jan 10
1E	Jason Henrichsen	Aug 12

1926 S

1B2	David Close	Aug 06
1I1	" "	July 09
1N	" "	Jan 10
1Q	John Vernieri	Jan 11
1S	Leroy Van Allen	May 12
1U	David Close	Mar 13
1V	" "	Mar 13
1W	" "	Mar 13
1Y	" "	July 13
2A	" "	Dec 04

1927 D

3A	Jeff Oxman	Feb 00

1927 S

1I	Bill Toland	Aug 11

1934 P

1A	David Close	Mar 07
1D	Bill Toland	Nov 11
1F	Coin World article	2012

1934 D

1C	Larry Briggs	Sep 10
2A	David Close	Jan 05

1935 P

1A	Larry Briggs	Oct 02
1B	Larry Briggs	Oct 02
1B2	James Cerny	Oct 10
1C	Bill Van Note	Jan 03

1935 S

3B	Ray Castro	Mar 13
5A	David Close	July 05

TYPES OF DIE GOUGES AND SCRATCHES

There are **hundreds** of different die **scratches** and **gouges** that have been reported over the years for the Peace dollar obverse and reverse dies. The **first one listed** as a VAM variety was reported in January 1974 by Bill Fivaz. It was a vertical die gouge from the D in GOD on a 1924 P and was assigned VAM 1A. As many more die gouges were reported, patterns and grouping began to unfold for these die scratches and gouges. Only recently have some of their causes been determined and investigated. Currently, they are broadly grouped by their cause as follows:

Feed Fingers Die Gouges & Beveled Fields	Unexplained Die Gouges & Scratches
Die Edges Gouges & Scratches	Special Extensive Gouges on Two 1923D Obverses

Some of these categories can be further divided for a total of **seven types** as indicated in the following paragraphs. Brief explanations of the various known causes of the gouges and scratches plus a couple example photographs are provided to familiarize the reader with the types of gouges and scratches that can be found on Peace dollars.

More detailed explanation of the causes along with listings of currently known VAM variety numbers and photographs are provided in the seven sections of the chapter, **Causes Of Die Gouges And Scratches.** A later chapter of **Die Gouges and Scratches Descriptive Listings**, describes all currently reported die gouges and scratches VAM varieties. **Appendices A** thru **D** provide photographs of all the currently known gouges and scratches die varieties for the four types that have more than just a few listings, i.e., feed fingers, die edge obverse and reverse and unexplained causes. Those causes that have only a few die varieties listed; Beveled Field, Double Die Edge Gouges and 1923 D Special Gouges, have all of their photographs included in their sections in the **Causes Of Die Gouges And Scratches** chapter.

Feed Fingers Die Gouges

These are **vertical gouges and scratches** on the **left and right sides** of the lower obverse dies. Sometimes they are accompanied by **flat shiny areas** that had been polished by extensive rubbing by feed finger flat bottom surfaces. The feed fingers are two flat steel arms that grab the planchets, advance forward to place the planchets over the lower die inside the collar hole while simultaneously pushing the struck coin off the raised lower die. Mis-adjustment and wear of the feed fingers mechanism can cause the feed fingers ends to contact the die fields that are the highest part of the lower die face. Repeated contact of the ends against the left or right fields can rub gouges into the die.

Examples of vertical feed finger die gouges on the lower left of the obverse die are shown for a **1923 P VAM 1G** and for the lower right side is shown for a **1922 P VAM 22A.**

Beveled Field From Feed Fingers

If the flat underside of either of the two feed fingers contact repeatedly the forward edge of the lower obverse die, then a shiny **beveled area next to the rim** can result. Again, this can happen when the lower die is raised slightly above the collar top to allow the struck coin to be pushed off. This would also be due to misadjustment or wear of the feed fingers and can occur on either the left or right side of the lower part of the obverse die from either the left or right feed finger. These beveled field areas should not be confused with beveled fields areas due to **over polishing** which are usually accompanied by die polishing or die file **<u>lines</u>** and are in other areas of the die, such as chin or hair top.

Only a few dies have been reported with beveled lower edges from feed fingers. Examples of one in the left side is for the **1922 P VAM 18** and one on the right side for the **1923 P VAM 1AB1.**

Die Edge Contact Gouges, Obverse

The Peace dollar dies had **two sharp edges** at the **rim notch**. The coining chamber of the coining presses were fairly confined with only a small distance between the upper and lower dies. During the installation of the top reverse die in the coining press by the die setter, if it was slightly tilted it could be **accidently contacted or brushed** against the lower obverse die top. This typically produced slightly **curved die gouge lines** with **tapered ends**. It was the **inner edge** of the rim that usually would contact the other die raised flat field when tilted at a slight angle from the vertical.

Quite few of these die edges gouges have been reported with most of the Philadelphia Mint. Examples are a **1923 P VAM 1G** with die edge gouge in rays below B and one high up thru E in LIBERTY of an **1923 P VAM 1K.**

Double Die Edge Contact Gouges

A few Peace dollar obverse dies show two fairly **closely spaced parallel short die gouges** or scratches. As shown in the chapter, **Measuring Die Rim Width And Depth**, the **inner** and **outer rim notch edges** of the upper reverse die can make **simultaneous** contact with the lower obverse die face when the upper die is tilted about 20° to 30° from the vertical. The **spacing** between the two parallel die gouges or scratches would be about **0.025" to 0.030"** to match the distance between the inner and outer die rim edges. Multiple contacts with the lower die produced several edges of double scratches.

This double die edge contact is a **rare occurrence** with only 10 reported or identified so far. The most prominent one is the **1922 P VAM 2N** with two strong parallel die gouges in the hair back of the eye. A possible multi-contact of double die edges is shown for the **1926 S VAM 1B2.**

Die Edge Contact Gouges, Reverse

There are possible die edge gouges on a number of upper reverse dies that are likely from contact of the lower obverse die as it was being installed in the coining press. Although fewer have been reported for the reverse die than the obverse die edge contact gouges, they are similar in appearance with **slightly curved or straight lines with tapered ends.** The upper reverse die had the entire die face well exposed when in the coining presses. So the lower obverse die edge contact could have occurred anywhere on the reverse raised die field face.

Examples are **1922 P VAM 2AE** with thin die gouge thru OL in DOLLAR and **1923 D VAM 1G** with thin die gouge well above DOLLAR.

Unexplained Die Gouges And Scratches

There are also quite a few die gouges and scratches on both the obverse and reverse dies that don't have the vertical orientation and lower obverse location of feed fingers die gouges or the fine line with tapered end gouges and scratches from the die edges. They instead are **short** and **broad** or **odd bent** and **curved shapes** that don't have a readily explanation of their causes.

A couple examples of unexplained causes of gouges and scratches are **1922 S VAM 2C1** flaming ray gouge, **1922 S VAM 2D** worm gouge thru G and **1923 P VAM 1AC1** with X die scratches below eagle's foot.

Special Extensive Gouges On Two 1923 D Obverses

Two obverse dies of **1923 D, VAMs 1BK and 1BS,** have unprecedented **extensive die gouges all over the obverse dies.** Apparently these two dies had their die faces together when in transit with their jostling together causing many fine and severe die gouges and scratches. The **VAM 1BK** has many die gouges on the Liberty head face and field in front of the nose plus an **amazing number** of gouges and scratches at L in LIBERTY. The **VAM 1BS** has very long die gouges from the rim below L in LIBERTY over across the Liberty head face. A couple photos are shown for each of these amazing die gouges Peace dollars!

1923 P VAM 1G Feed Fingers Gouges, Left

1922 P VAM 22A Feed Fingers Gouges, Right

1922 P VAM 18B Feed Fingers Beveled Field, Left

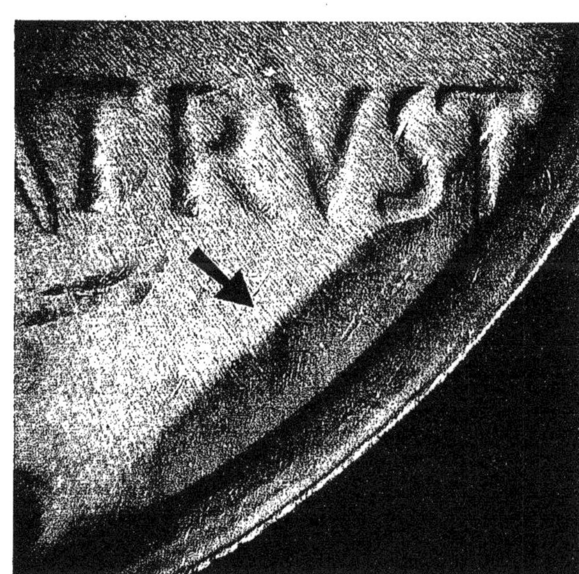

1923 P VAM 1AB1 Feed Fingers Beveled Field, Right

1923 P VAM 1G Die Edge Gouge Below B

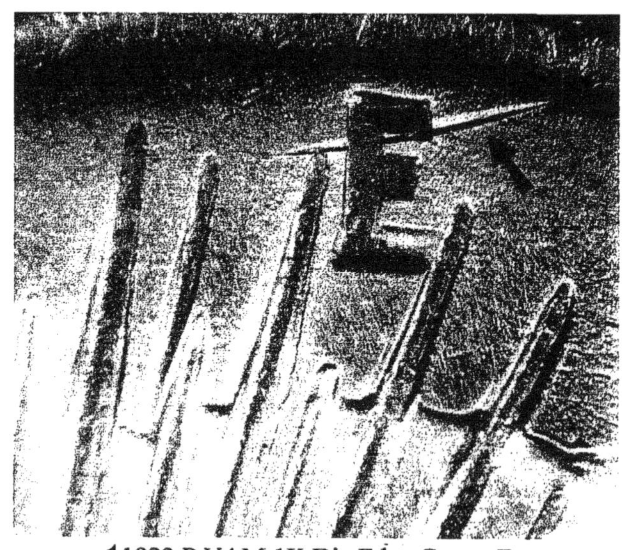

1923 P VAM 1K Die Edge Gouge E

1922 P VAM 2N Double Die Edge Gouges

1923 D VAM 1G Die Edge Gouge Rays

1923 P VAM 1AC1 X Die Scratches

1926 S VAM 1B2 Multiple Double Die Edge Gouges

1922 P VAM 2AE Die Edge Gouge DOLL

1922 S VAM 2C Flaming Ray Die Gouge

1922 S VAM 2D Curved Die Gouge G

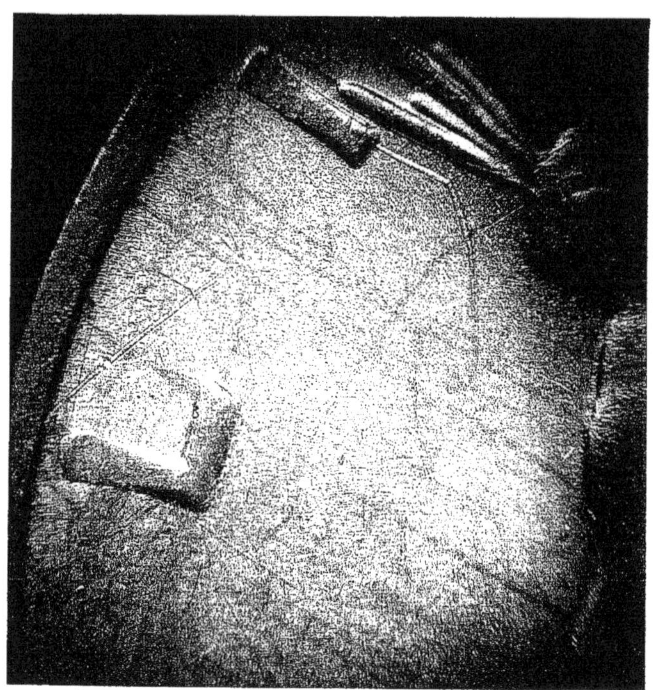
1923 D VAM 1BK Die Gouges/Scratches LI

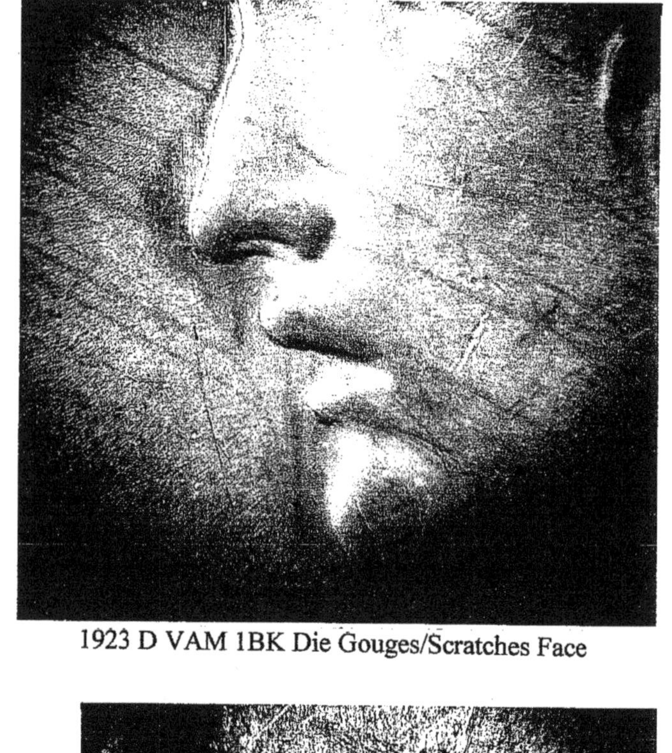
1923 D VAM 1BK Die Gouges/Scratches Face

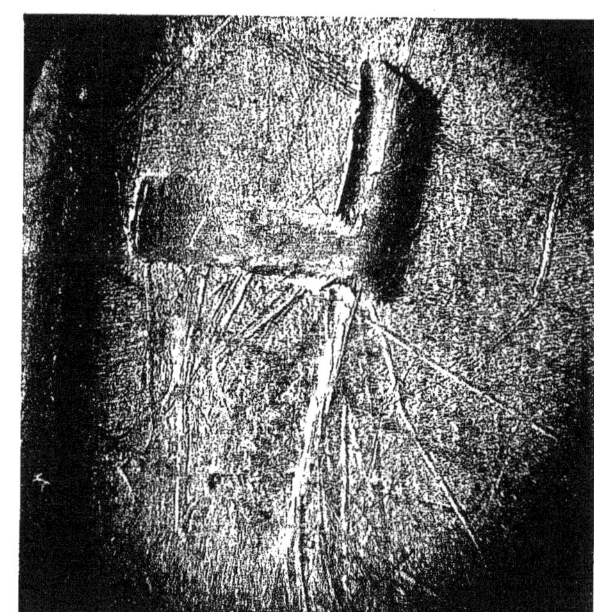
1923 D VAM 1BK Die Gouges/Scratches L

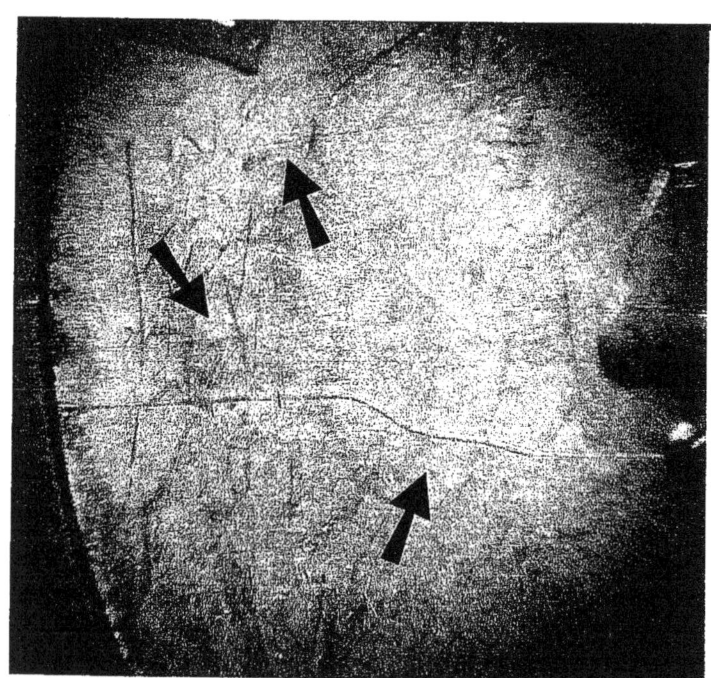
1923 D VAM 1BS Die Gouge & Scratch

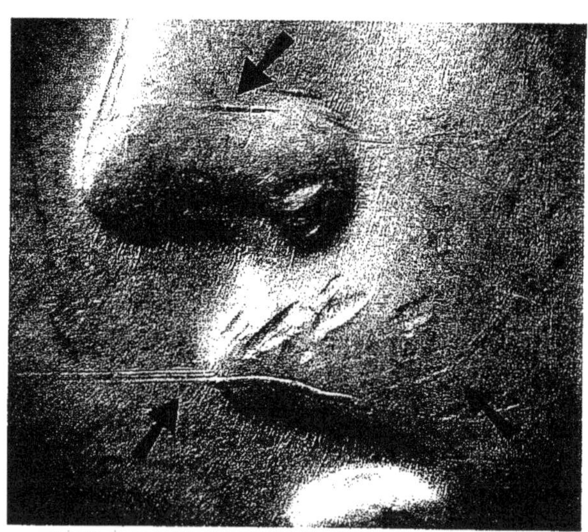
1923 D VAM 1BS Hooked Liberty Lip Gouge

CAUSES OF DIE GOUGES AND SCRATCHES

This chapter treats the **seven categories** of the **causes of die gouges and scratches** on Peace dollar dies. These are covered the following sections:

- Feed Fingers Die Gouges
- Beveled Field From Feed Fingers
- Die Edge Contact Gouges, Obverse
- Double Die Edge Contact Gouges
- Die Edge Contact Gouges, Reverse
- Die Gouges And Scratches Without Specific Cause
- 1923 D Special Cases of Two Obverses Die Gouges

Each possible cause is examined in detail in separate sections that includes **where** the gouges and scratches are likely to occur on the dies, their **differences** in size and orientation and **why** they occur. Listings of all the currently reported VAM numbers for die varieties of gouges and scratches are provided along with some example photographs of the different types of die gouges and scratches.

More detailed **descriptions** of each die gouge variety is provided in the chapter on **Die Gouges And Scratches Descriptive Listings.** **Photographs** of all the different VAM numbered die varieties are provided in **Appendices A thru D** for **feed finger** types in **Appendix A, die edge** gouges on **obverse** in **Appendix B, die edge** gouges on **reverse** in **Appendix C** and **unexplained** die gouges in **Appendix D.** The other die gouge categories of **beveled field, double die edge** and the **two 1923 D obverses** have all their reported die variety photographs in their respective sections in this chapter since they have only a few.

Feed Fingers Die Gouges

It has been very strange that only vertical die gouges are mostly found on the lower left and right obverse and primarily for the Philadelphia Mint dies. A likely cause of these die gouges were the **feed finger ends repeatedly contacting the lower obverse die fields** during the striking of the coins in the coining presses.

This is a **similar** cause of die gouges and polished areas that occurred on the **top** of the **lower reverse** Morgan dollar dies. The feed fingers sometimes contacted the fields near the top of the Morgan dollar reverse dies above the eagle's wing tips. The die top must have been facing outwards in the coining press with the top obverse die in the normal upright position to produce struck coins in the usual viewing position.

Contemporary Coining Presses

One of the questions is, **what kind of coining presses** and their **feed fingers** were in use during the striking of Peace dollars from 1921 thru 1935. Unfortunately the author has no access for coining presses photographs specifically identified as in use for those years. However, the Peace dollars were initially struck in 1921, only 17 years after the regular Morgan dollar production ended in 1904. A couple accompanying photographs show the **large coining press** in use at the **Philadelphia Mint in 1901** with a close-up photograph of the feed fingers area. At that time the planchets were hand fed into a tube for the feed finger pick-up. Another photograph of the No. 1 coining press for the Carson City Mint shows a **similar design press** that had later been modified for automatic feeding of the planchets in the close-up photograph. This type of coining press was **still in use in the 1950s** as shown in another photograph also with automatic planchet feeder.

Another photograph shows a smaller coining press in use at the Philadelphia Mint in 1896 for striking of minor coins with a **clearer photograph** of the feed fingers and upper die between them. Several **drawings of the large coining press** from the *U.S. Treasury Department, Annual Report of the Director of the Mint 1902* show the front and side views with another illustration showing an enlargement of just the feed fingers and dies area, with the collar surrounding the lower die.

Coining Press Operation

The **upper die**, D, was the **reverse** for the Peace dollar from 1922 onwards. It was fastened to the triangle which moved up and down. The **lower obverse die**, C, was fastened to the die stake. Over the die state was the collar, B, into which the planchets dropped and produced the reeding on the coin edges when it was struck. The planchets dropped from the tube, A, into the **two flat steel feed fingers**, G. They were then carried between the dies and dropped onto the collar and onto of the lower die when the steel feed fingers expanded. The manually fed planchet tube by the coining press operator was later replaced by automatic planchet feed mechanisms that were likely in place by the 1920s.

After the coin was stuck, the press toggle joint was bent **raising the upper die one-half inch** above the collar. The die stake with the **lower die was raised slightly about one-eighth of an inch** forcing the newly struck coin up out of the collar. This coin was forced off the lower die by the **front of the advancing closed feed fingers** carry the next planchet. **It was at this time** that the **front of the feed fingers could contact** the **raised lower die** if they were not properly adjusted or there was wear on the blocks that the feed fingers slid on or wear on the bottom of the feed fingers.

The back and forth movement of the feed fingers could wear **straight parallel groves** in the lower die from **repeated contact**. Most of these die gouges are on the lower obverse of the Peace dollar that was the side closest to the initial overriding of the feed fingers.

Feed Fingers and Collar

Separate photographs show an actual 1966 quarter canceled die and collar which was very similar to these pieces used to strike the Peace dollars. Another two photographs show actual feeder fingers (more commonly known as feed fingers), collar and surrounding collar holder for dual 10 cent in use in 1973. That shows how **flat the feed fingers** were and the **ends that pushed the struck coins** off the raised lower die.

Photographs of simulated quarter collar and die shows the die in a retracted and the raised positions for the feed finger ends to push the struck coin off the lower dies. The collar rests on springs as shown in a 1977 die press holder and die fixture at the Philadelphia Mint. A couple other photographs show a quarter press of 1977 with feed fingers, collar holder, and collar. Another photograph shows a cent press with planchets in position for feed fingers pick-up of 1988. These photographs should show the reader the mechanism complexity of the feed fingers and die operation in a coining press.

Feed Fingers Operation

The feed fingers are **two long flat steel bars** as previously shown that **pivot** in the open and closed positions to grip the planchet. Their operation is shown in the accompanying diagram and is briefly as follows. A **semi-circular opening** on the forward end of each bar closes to grasp a planchet dropped onto them. The Peace dollar upper reverse die rises above the collar and the **lower obverse die raises slightly** above the collar **pushing the struck coin out of the collar**. Then the feed fingers **advance** in a closed position, **pushing the coin off the raised lower die** and into a hopper at the rear of the coining press. The lower die then retracts and the feed fingers then open dropping the planchet into the collar over the obverse die and retracts to grasp the next planchet. The upper reverse hammer die then comes down striking the coin inside the collar to impart the obverse and reverse design and edge reeding.

Normally the feed fingers were not near the retracted lower and upper dies. The only time they were close was when the **feed fingers were closed and pushed the struck coin off** the slightly raised lower die. It was at that time that the **feed finger ends could have scraped across the lower Peace dollar obverse die** that was slightly raised above the collar, if the coin press was not properly adjusted or parts worn. This is shown in the enlarged drawing of how the feed fingers would contact the raised lower die. The depth and extent of the gouges would depend on the **amount of mis-adjustment or wear** on the feed fingers bottom that allowed the feed fingers to contact the lower die face plus the **number of times** the feed fingers end scraped across the die face. The much scarcer occurrence of **beveled lower obverse fields** was likely caused by the **flat forward underneath part of the feed fingers repeatedly** sliding across the lower die forward edge. These beveled fields are treated in a separate section.

Why Philadelphia Mint Had Most Gouges

By far, the largest number of feed fingers obverse die gouges occurred on the Philadelphia Mint dies of 92. Of course the Philadelphia Mint struck the most Peace dollar coins from 1921 thru 1926 of about 100 million. But over 50 million San Francisco Mint coins and almost 25 million Denver Mint coins were struck during the same time period. Only 11 San Francisco Mint feed fingers die gouge varieties have bee reported to date and only 13 for the Denver Mint dies. Either the Philadelphia Mint coining presses were often out of adjustment and worn or their different design more often allowed the feed fingers contact with the lower obverse die. There are two possible feed finger die gouges in the lower reverse dies of the 1921 Peace dollar, which had the dies in opposite positions than from 1922 and later.

Reported Feed Fingers Die Gouges

Vertical die gouges on the lower part of the Peace dollar obverse dies have been known since a particularly strong one from the D in GOD for the **1924 P VAM 1A** was **first reported by Bill Fivaz** in **January 1974.** The other vertical die gouge on the lower obverse listed early and pictured in the

VAM book was the **1923 P VAM 1F** reported by **Jon Steinberg in July 1982.**

There are currently **116** listed Peace dollar die varieties with vertical die gouges on the lower obverse and a few on the upper obverse. They vary in widths and location, primarily on the lower left and lower right sides. Some show only a single vertical die gouge while quite a few show multiple closely grouped vertical die gouges. The gouges can be a single bar, closely spaced bars or single lines along with flat polished bands. The vast majority die gouges are the **92** for the **Philadelphia Mint** years from 1921 thru 1926 with the most, **34** for the 1922 P. Only **13** die gouges are listed for **Denver Mint** years of 1922 D, 1923 D, 1926 D and 1934 D that are fairly weak. There are **11** listed for the **San Francisco Mint** years of 1922 S, 1923 S, 1926 S and 1935 S.

The following are the all the reported feed fingers die gouge varieties listed to date, along with some example photographs. **Appendix A, Feed Fingers Die Gouges**, show photographs of all the currently reported die gouges from feed fingers.

1921 Peace VAMs 1E2, 1J
1922 P VAMs 1B, 1D, 1H, 1P, 1Q, 1U, 2E, 2F, 2J, 2M, 2P, 2R, 2S, 2W, 2Z, 2AX, 2BL, 2CC, 2CQ, 2CR, 2CU, 2CW, 2DD, 2DE, 2DM, 2DQ, 5-2, 5A1, 5C, 25B, 29A, 31A, 34A, 54A
1922 D VAMs 2W, 5
1922 S VAMs 1A, 2AI
1923 P VAMs 1C, 1F, 1G, 1N, 1U, 1X, 1AD, 1AI, 1AS, 1BA, 1BF, 1BM, 1BO, 1BR, 1BT, 1BY, 1CB, 1CC, 1CH, 7A
1923 D VAMs 1D1, 1AG, 1AX1, 1BI, 1BK1, 1CC, 1CE, 1CF
1923 S VAMs 1BX, 1CP, 1CR
1924 P VAMs 1A1, 1E, 1F, 1K1, 1L, 1M, 1N, 1O, 1S, 1U, 1Y, 1Z, 1AI, 1AJ, 1AL, 1AR, 1AU, 1AV, 1BT
1925 P VAMs 1B, 1D, 1E, 1F, 1S, 1AA, 1AD, 1AE, 1AM, 1AN, 2A, 9A, 11A, 18A
1926 P VAMs 1C1, 3A, 4A
1926 D VAM 1E
1926 S VAMs 1S, 1U, 1V, 1W, 1Y
1934 D VAMs 1C, 2A
1935 S VAM 3B

1923 P VAM 1F1 Chin Bar Die Gouge

1924 P VAM 1A1 Bar D

Coining Press, 1901, Philadelphia Mint
(Director of the Mint Annual Report, 1902)

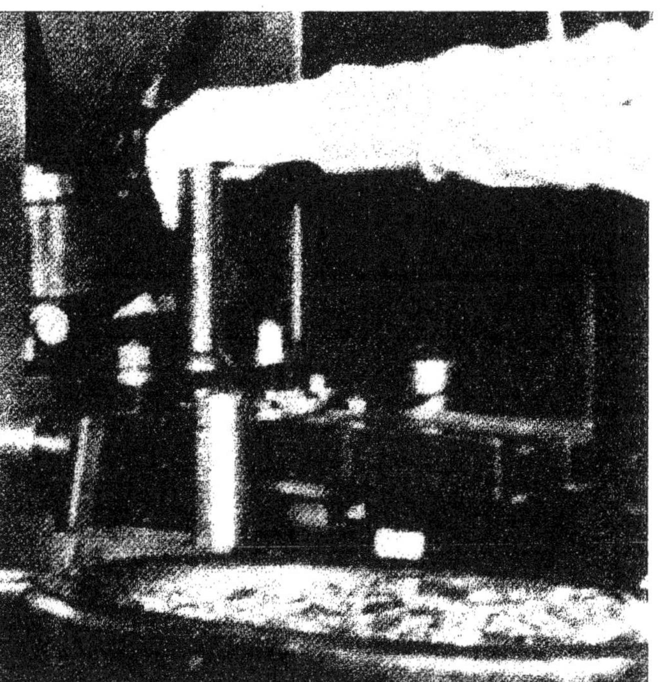

Coining Press, Feed Fingers, Philadelphia Mint, 1901
(Director of the Mint Annual Report, 1902)

Small Coining Press, 1896, Showing Feed Fingers
(Director of the Mint Annual Report, 1896)

Small Coining Press, 1896, Feed Fingers & Die
(Director of the Mint Annual Report, 1896)

Carson City Press Feed Fingers Tracks
(Early 1970s)

Cent Press With Planchets in Position for Feed Fingers Pick-up
(Philadelphia Mint 1988)

Coining Press, 1950s, With Automatic Planchet Feed
(Photo courtesy The U.S. Mint and Coinage, Don Taxay)

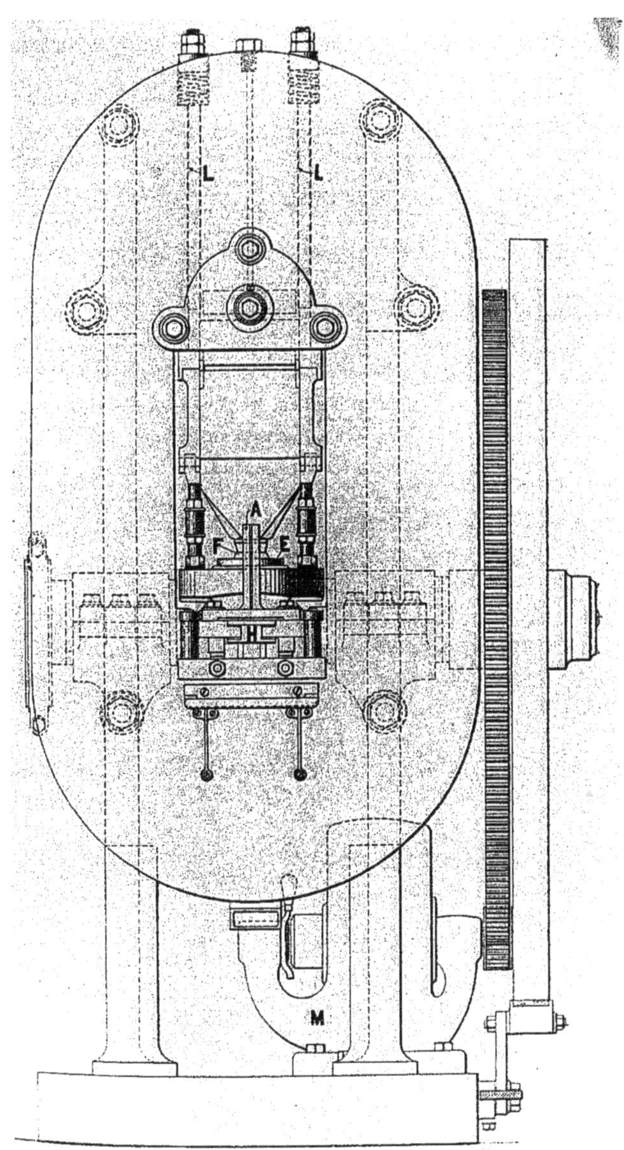

Coin Press Drawing, 1901, Front View
(U.S. Treasury Dept, Annual Report of the Director of the Mint, 1902)

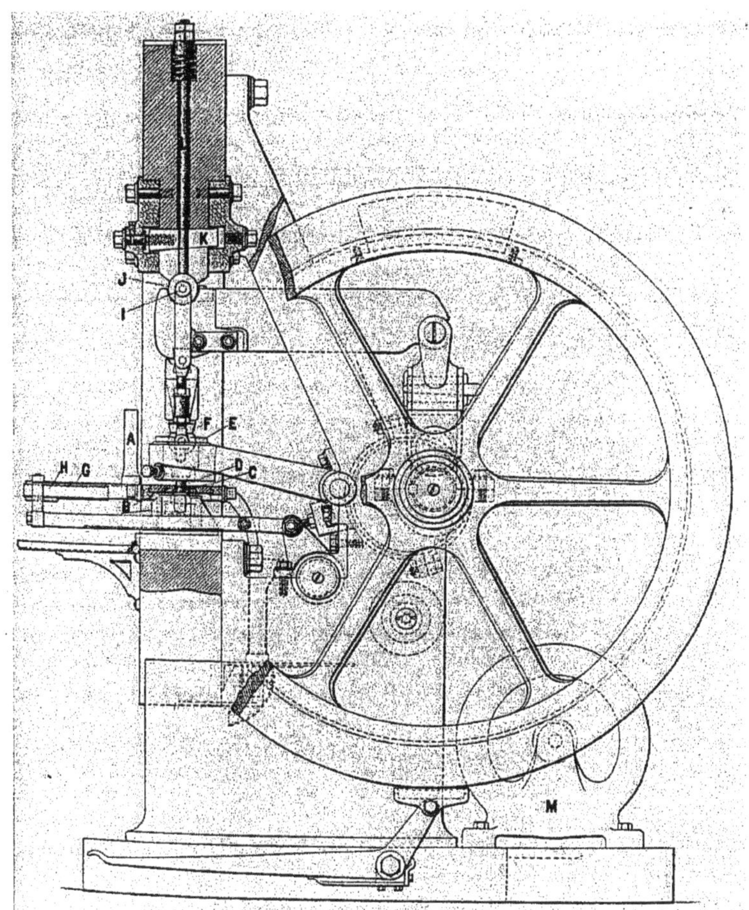

Coin Press Drawing, 1901, Side View
(Director of the Mint Annual Report, 1902)

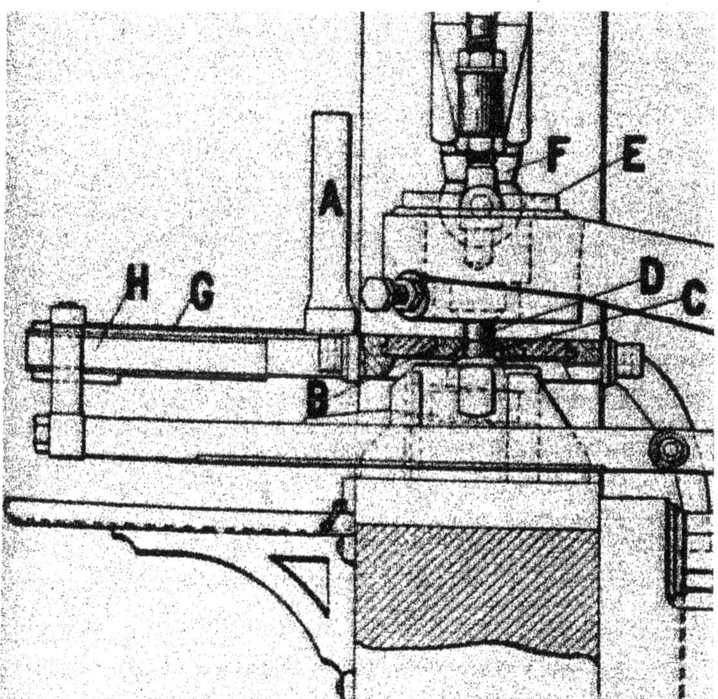

Coin Press, 1901, Side View, Feed Fingers & Dies
(Director of the Mint Annual Report, 1902)

No. 1 Press For Carson City Mint
(Early 1970s)

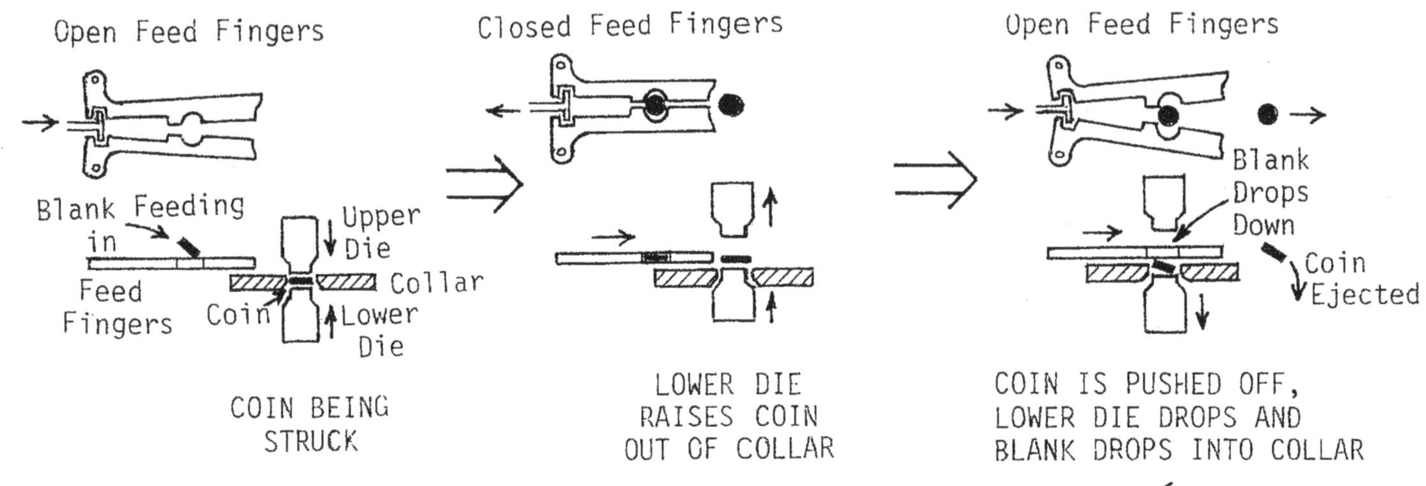

Feed Fingers and Die Operation

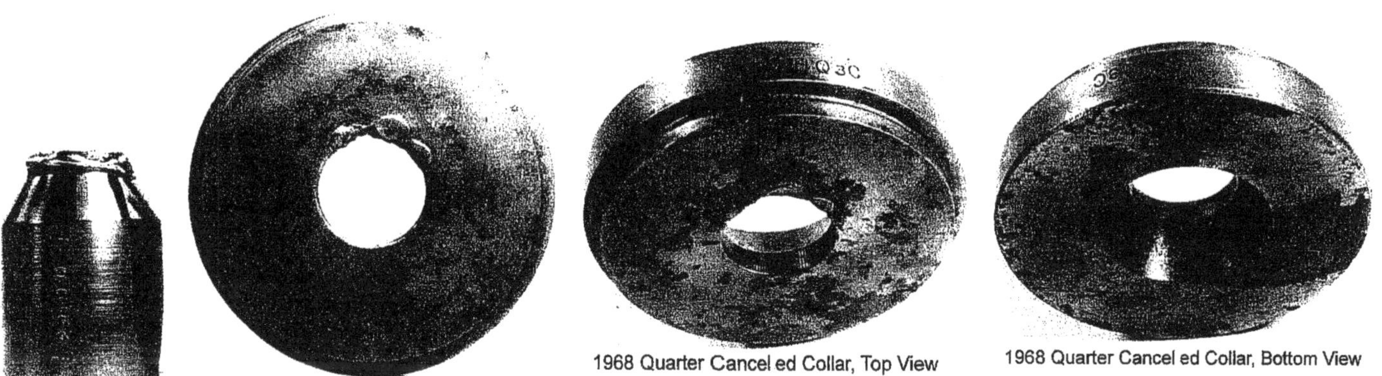

1968 Quarter Canceled Die & Collar

1968 Quarter Cancel ed Collar, Top View

1968 Quarter Cancel ed Collar, Bottom View

Dual 10 Cent Feed Fingers, Collar & Collar Holder
(Photo courtesy Alan Herbert, Philadelphia Mint, 1973)

Dual 10 Cent Feed Fingers Over Collar & Collar Holder
(Photo courtesy Alan Herbert, Philadelphia Mint 1973)

Simulated Quarter Collar & Retracted Die

Simulated Quarter Collar With Raised Die

Press Holder & Die Fixture With Collar Springs
(Philadelphia Mint 1977)

Quarter Press With Collar & Collar Holder Below Upper Die Holder
(Photo courtesy Alan Herbert, Philadelphia Mint 1973)

Quarter Press With Feed Fingers Rear & Upper Die Ram
(Photo courtesy Alan Herbert, Philadelphia Mint 1973)

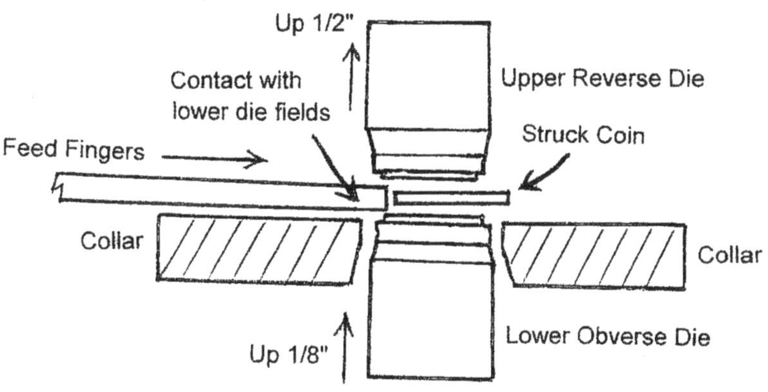

Coin Ejection & Feed Finger Contact of Lower Die Fields
(Press Side View)

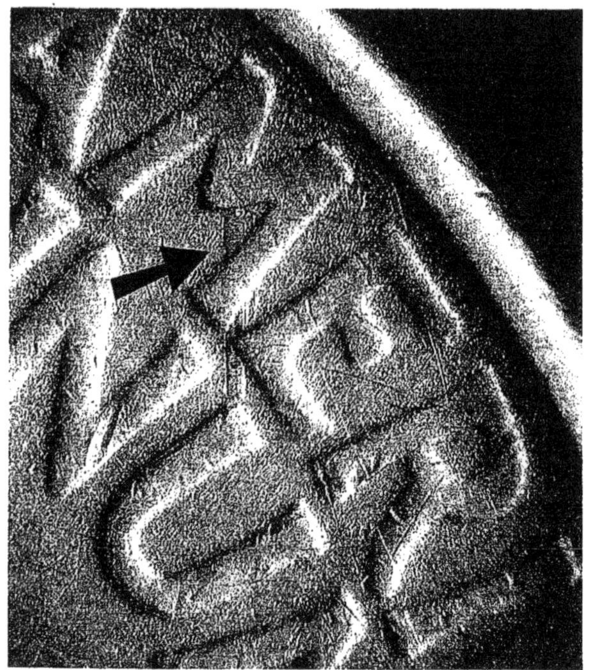

1921 VAM 1E2 Die Gouge MEU

1922 P VAM 2E Vertical Gouge 19

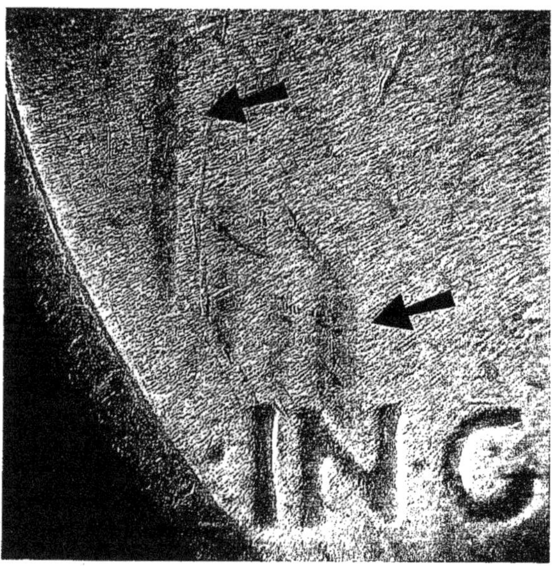

1922 P VAM 2S Triple Gouges

1922 P VAM 31A Gouges Above IN

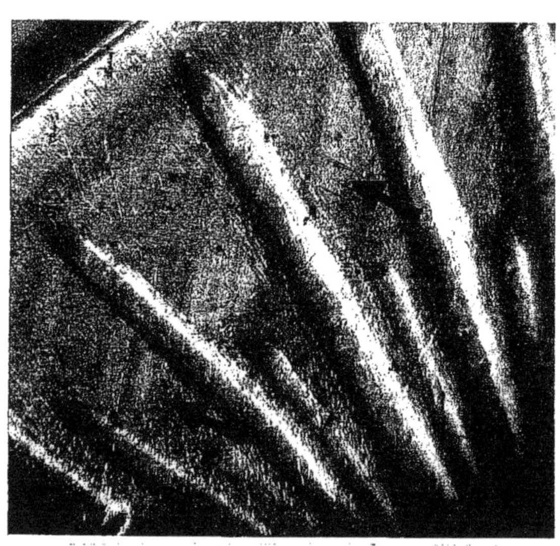

1922 S VAM 2AI Gouges Front Rays

1922 S VAM 1A Die Gouge I

1923 P VAM 1G Die Gouge O

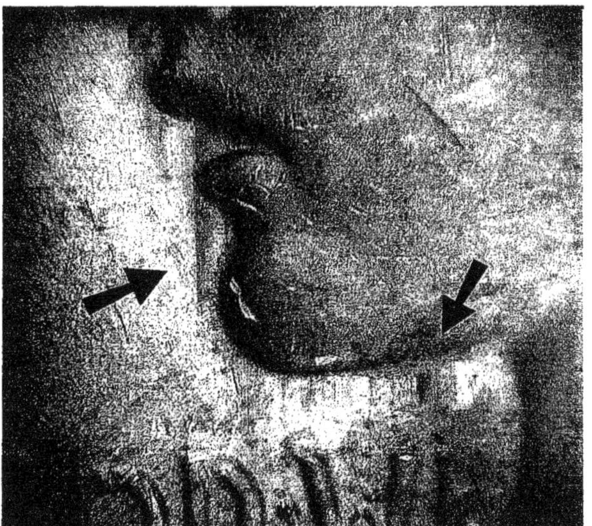

1923 D VAM 1CF Gouges Lips & Jaw

1924 P VAM 1Z Gouge Right of G

1923 P VAM 1AS Gouge Thru RV

1924 P VAM 1N Gouge S

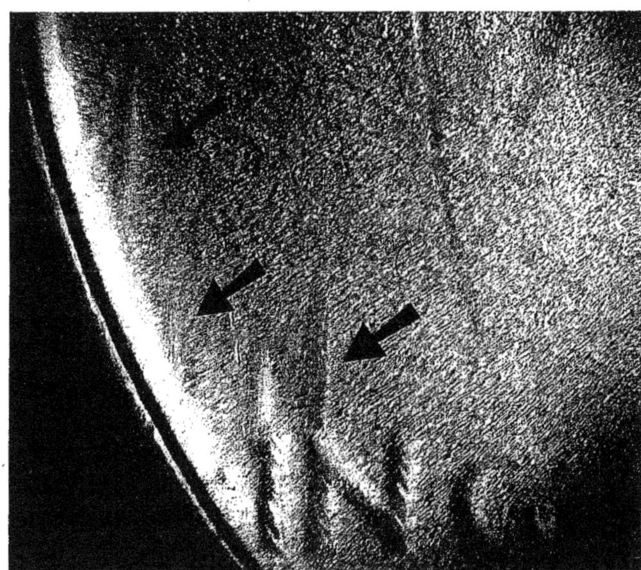

1925 P VAM 1AE Four Gouges Above IN

Beveled Field From Feed Fingers

A few Peace dollar die varieties show a **beveled field** that is **tilted and smooth** with **shiny tops at the rim** of the **lower obverse die**. It is strange that they only appear at this one location. The cause is likely multiple contacts with the **feed fingers** that **wore down and polished these edges** of the Peace dollar lower obverse dies. They are **related to the vertical gouges** and polished bands that appear on the lower portions of the obverse die from the feed finger contact as previously explained. The bottom face of the obverse die must have been facing outward in the coining presses and closest to the feed fingers that operated at the coining presses front.

These beveled fields were produced by the **repeated contacts** with the **flat portion of the feed finger bars** instead of the feed fingers ends that produced the gouge lines and bars in the same areas. These polished and beveled fields are related to the polished areas at the top of the Morgan dollar reverse dies that were the lower die in the coining presses. In the case of the Morgan dollar reverse dies, their top must have been facing outwards in the coining presses.

There are **other instances of beveled fields** that are the **result of over polished dies**. They are most frequent at the forward hair edge of the Liberty head on the obverse die, and were attempts to remove die clash marks there. Usually there are the **straight closely spaced die file lines** at the beveled field or in the nearby fields. This clearly identifies the beveled field as the result of die polishing and not due to feed fingers scraping repeatedly at die edges. Most of these beveled fields from die over polishing were performed by the San Francisco Mint and show at the forward hair edge, top of hair below R and below the Liberty head jaw on the obverse dies.

The earliest reported beveled field caused by the feed fingers contact was the **1923 P VAM 1Z revision** reported by **Robert Varoe in March 2006.** This was followed by the **1922 P VAM 18 revision** by **Michael Ash in September 2006.**

The following are lists and photographs reported so far for the nine beveled fields on the lower obverse of the Peace dollar that were caused by the flat surface of the feed fingers. All nine are of the Philadelphia Mint. Perhaps a coining press there had defective feed fingers that allowed repeated contact with the obverse die edge.

1922 P VAMs 2BZ, 2CX, 18revision, 22A
1923 P VAMs 1Zrevision, 1AB1, 1BG, 1CF, 4A

1922 P VAM 1BZ Beveled Field

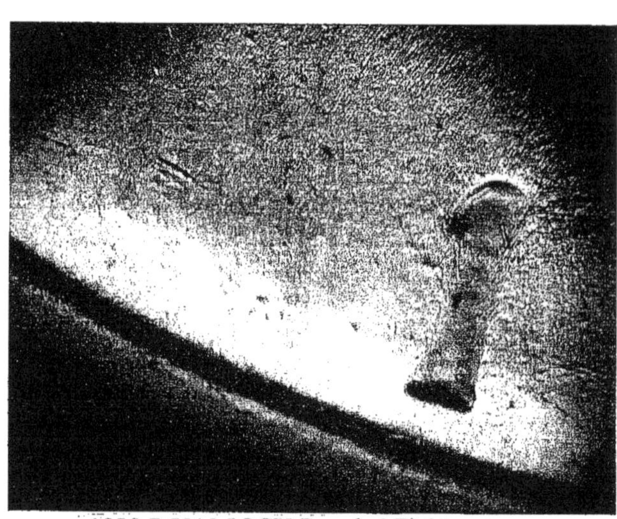

1922 P VAM 2CX Beveled Field at 1

1922 P VAM 18B Beveled Field

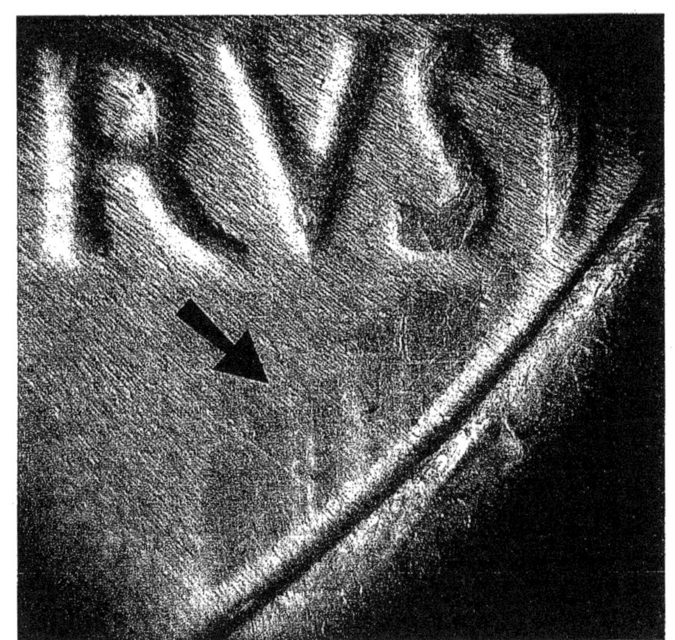

1922 P VAM 22A Beveled Rim, Multiple Gouges

1923 P VAM 1Z Damaged Beveled Field TRVST

1923 P VAM 1AB1 Beveled Field

1923 P VAM 1BG Beveled Field Below 23

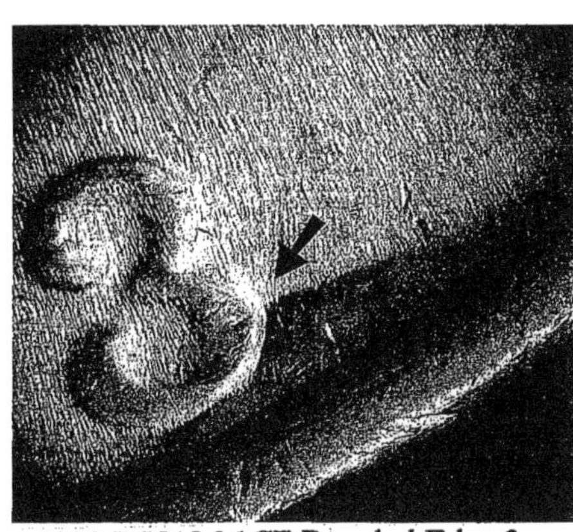

1923 P VAM 1CF Beveled Edge 3

1923 P VAM 4A Beveled Field Below RVST, Rt. Of T

Die Edge Contact Gouges, Obverse

It is very **unusual** that the Peace dollar obverse dies have quite a number of **thin medium length die gouges and scratches in the Liberty head rays**. There are a few similar thin gouges all over the reverse dies. It is thought that these are due to contact of the upper reverse die edge as they were being installed in the coining press.

Similar Morgan Dollar Reverse Gouges

The **equivalent strange** die markings for the Morgan dollar reverse dies are primarily on the bottom areas since they were the lower die. The top of the Morgan dollar reverse dies was closest to the front of the coining presses. These markings have been attributed to the **edge denticle impressions of the inside rim of the upper Morgan die** that was accidently brushed or fell against the lower reverse die face **as the dies were being installed in the coining press**. The triangle shaped raised dots in a short line have the same spacing as the denticle spaces of the obverse Morgan die. A few of these reverse Morgan dies show **rows of triangle denticle impressions with a parallel die edge gouge 0.025" below**. A prominent example is the illustrated 1881 O VAM 18A with both denticle and die edge impressions. **This is proof of the die edge contact**. Over 47 Morgan dollar dies with these denticle impressions have been reported so far. Because the dies were hardened when installed in the coining presses, only another hardened die would have made these denticle impressions.

Peace Dollar Dies

The Peace dollar dies of course did not have denticles next to the rim. However, the rim had a **very sharp edge** at the **very outside of the die face** and **another sharp edge at the inside** of the rim notch. See the accompanying photograph of an Ike dollar die face that was similar to the Peace dollar dies face. The Ike dollar dies were one and one-half inches in diameter, length of about two and one-quarter inches and weighed about one and one-half pounds.

The chapter on **Measuring Die Rim Width And Depth** provides likely Peace dollar die shape and dimensions that were similar to the Morgan dollar dies. They were two inches long and one and three quarters inches in diameter. The raised rim was measured on a number of Peace dollar coins and is 0.025" in radial extent and 0.010" high, as detailed in this separate chapter. It was the **inside edge of the rim notch** in the reverse die that **caused most of the die edge gouges and scratches** on the top of the obverse dies. The reverse die had to be tilted beyond 25° to 30° from the vertical position to have just the outside edge contact the lower obverse as shown in the diagram in the Measuring Die Rim Width And Depth chapter. This was likely a rare occurrence.

This corresponds to the Morgan dollar inner denticle impressions only cases on the lower reverse die being more frequent than the denticle impressions with adjacent outside die edge contact line gouge or infrequent just the outside die edge gouges.

Die Installation In Coining Presses

There was very limited space between the upper reverse die and the lower obverse die and surrounding collar in the coining presses at the time the Peace dollars were struck. The space between the dies was fairly small as shown in the photographs for the die chamber for the No. 1 Press for the Carson City Mint. This type coining press was likely still in use during the 1920's when the Peace dollar was struck. Other photographs show the coining chamber of two 1970s presses that was still fairly confined.

The die setter had to carefully place the upper reverse die above and close to the lower obverse die during it's installation in order to insert it into the hole in the upper triangle and lock it in place with large set screws. If the upper reverse die was **slightly tilted** during its placement over the lower die and **low enough to accidently contact** the lower obverse die, a die gouge or scratch would result. This is illustrated in the **accompanying diagram** that shows how the inner edge of the rim edge on the top die could contact the lower recessed die if accidently placed too low and to the rear with a slight tilt during the die installation.

Causes of Die Gouges And Scratches

With the hardened dies that were installed in the coining presses, **only another hardened die** could have produced the thin medium length die gouges on the upper part of the lower obverse die. Since the bottom of some obverse dies have vertical feed finger gouges that faced outwards in coining presses, the **top of the obverse die was at the back of coining chamber** in the coining presses

A **sharp inner die edge** of the upper reverse die would cause a **slightly curved thin die gouge with tapered ends** if hit directly or accidentally fell down on the lower obverse die. A **brushing sideways** would produce a **straight line thin gouge**. With a weight of around one and one-half pounds, the reverse Peace dollar die could drop on the lower die with considerable force. Most of these thin gouges occurred in the top field, but a few are in the upper letters, hair and face of the obverse die.

The conclusion is that the **thin slightly curved and with tapered ends gouge or scratches** at the **top of the lower obverse die** of the Peace dollars was likely accidently caused by a **slight tilt** and **contact or brushing against the lower obverse die face** by the **inside rim edge** of the **upper reverse die during it's installation.**

Reported Die Edge Gouges

Currently, **61 obverse Peace dollar dies** have been reported with these **thin die edge** gouges and scratches on the obverse die. Included are three 1921 Peace dollar reverse dies which were the lower die as proven by collar clash impressions on the obverse hammer die. Most of the reported die edge contact gouges are in the rays of the Liberty head top in a horizontal or slightly diagonal direction. The **first reported thin die gouge** in the rays was for the **1922 P VAM 2F** reported by **Leroy Van Allen in February 1983. Jeff Oxman** reported the **next two in February 1998** for the **1922 P VAM 2H** and **1923 P VAM 1G**.

Most of these **61** die edge gouges and scratches occurred on the **Philadelphia Mint dies** with **42.** There are **10** for the **San Francisco Mint dies** and **9** for the **Denver Mint dies.** Of course the Philadelphia Mint struck about twice as many Peace dollar coins as the San Francisco Mint and about four times that of the Denver Mint. But there is still a disproportionate number of Philadelphia Mint die edge gouges during 1922 and 1923. Perhaps this was due to different coining press design with closer coining chamber, or not as careful die installer.

The following lists all the currently reported die edge gouges and scratches die varieties along with some example die edge contact gouges shown in the accompanying photographs. **Appendix B, Die Edge Gouges On Obverse** shows photographs of all the currently reported obverse die edge contact gouges.

1921 Peace VAMs 1E, 1T, 1X
1922 P VAMs 1A, 1C, 1X, 2F, 2H, 2K, 2X, 2Y, 2AC, 2AI, 2AK, 2AL, 2AS/AG, 2AW, 2BJ, 2BO, 2BQ, 2DG, 2DQ
1922 D VAMs 1F, 1P, 2BJ, 2BO, 7
1922 S VAMs 2I, 2Z, 5A
1923 P VAMs 1G, 1J, 1K, 1L, 1M, 1P, 1R, 1AG, 1AM, 1AO, 1BH, 1BS
1923 D VAMs 1V, 1AN
1923 S VAMs 1AO, 1BW
1924 P VAMs 1AD, 1AS, 1AT, 1AY, 1BE, 8B
1924 S VAMs 1C, 1L
1925 P VAMs 1A, 1AB
1925 S VAMs 1A1, 1A2
1926D VAM 1C
1926 S VAM 1N
1927 D VAM 3A

Morgan Dollar 1881 O VAM 18A Denticle Impressions & Die Edge Gouge

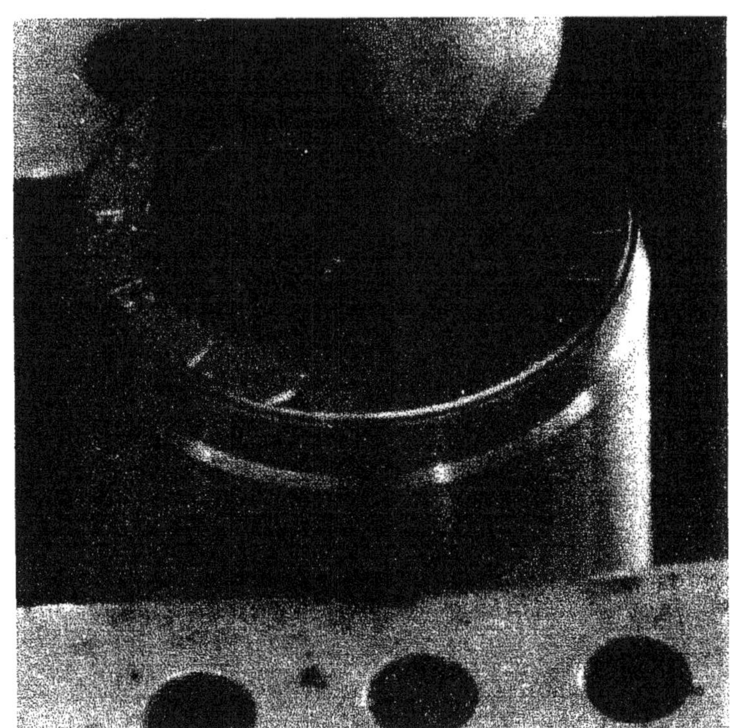
Ike Dollar Die Shape

No. 1 Press For Carson City Mint

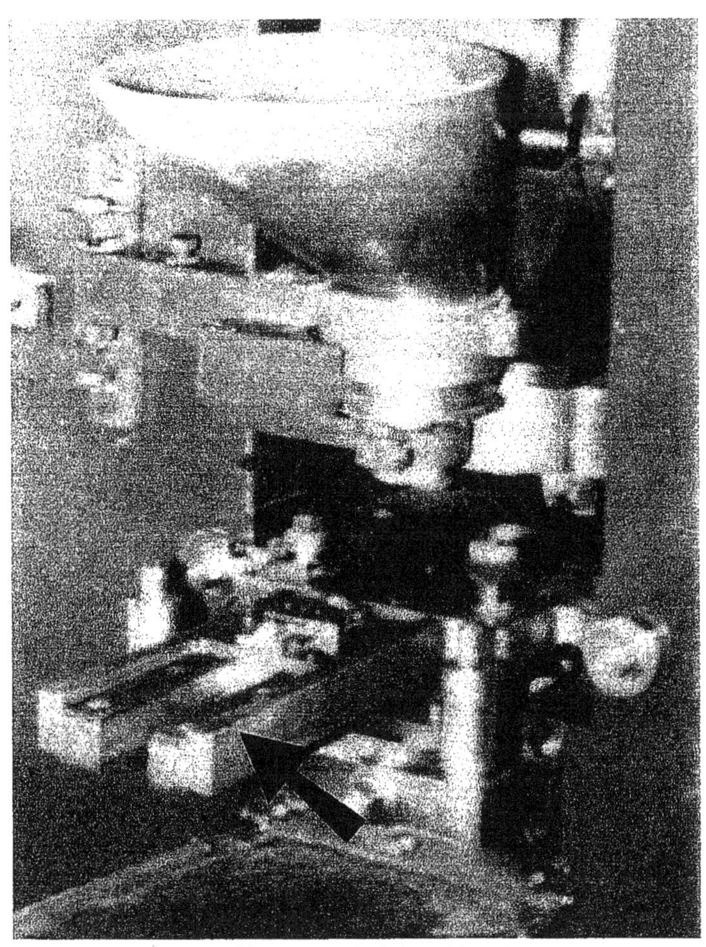
Carson City Press Coining Chamber

Quarter Press Showing Coining Chamber, 1973

Feed Fingers & Upper Die in Press, 1970s

Close-up of Feed Fingers & Upper Die Holder, 1970s

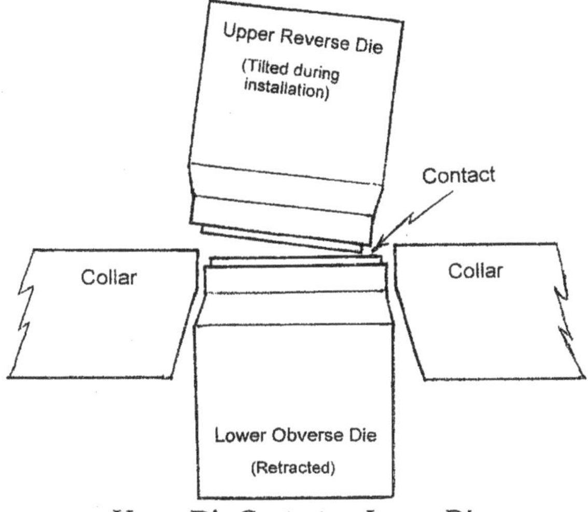

Upper Die Contact on Lower Die
(Press side view)

1922 VAM 1A Die Gouge Rays

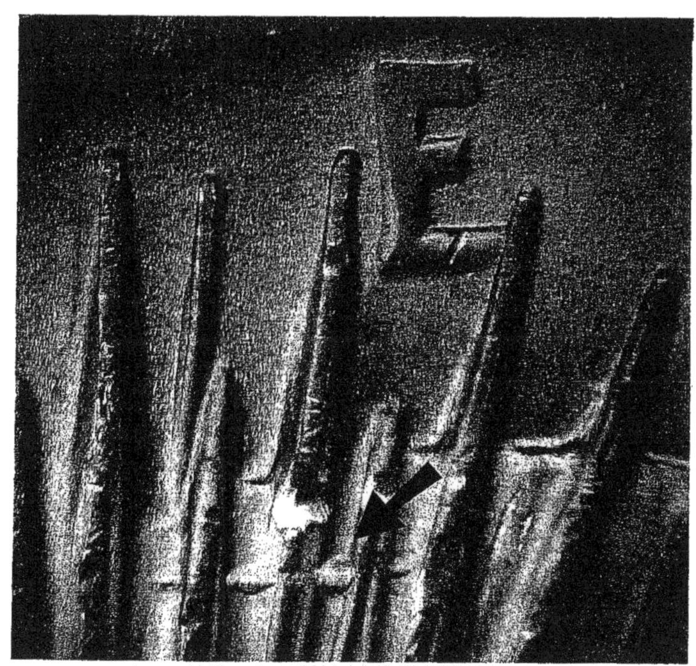
1922 P VAM 2F Die Gouge Below E

1922 P VAM 2H Die Gouge Below B

1922 P VAM 2AL Die Gouge Jaw

1922 P VAM 1BO Die Scratch WE

1922 P VAM 2DG Die Gouges Cheek

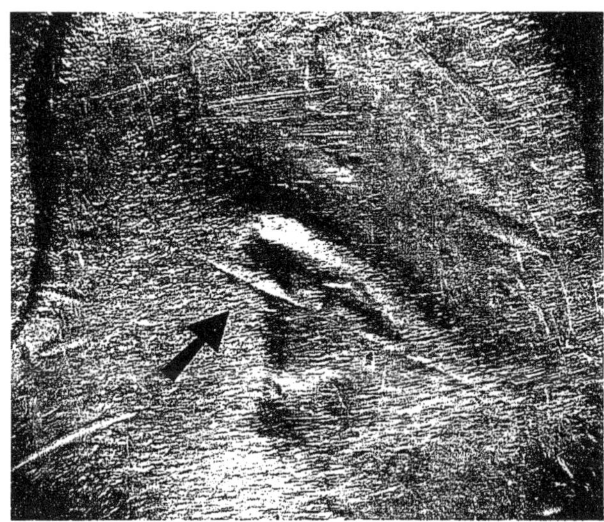
1922 D VAM 1F Spiked Eye Die Gouge

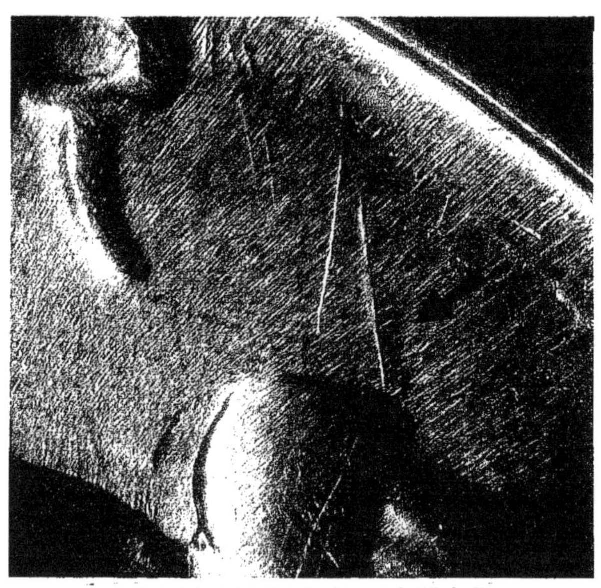
1922 S VAM 2Z Die Scratch Hair Bun

1923 P VAM 1G Die Gouge Below B

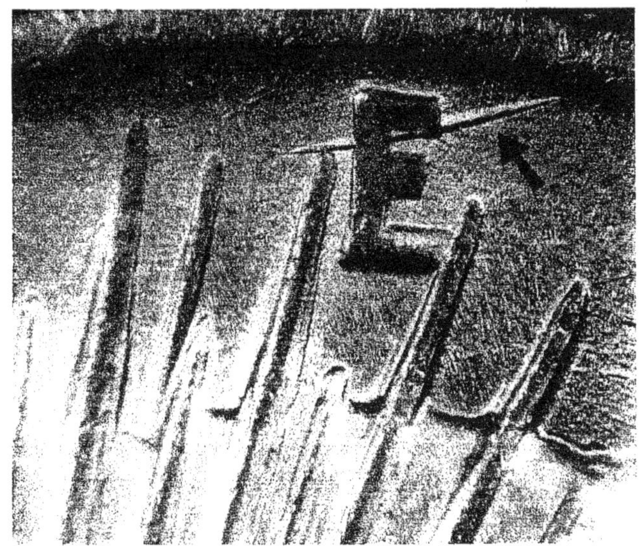

1923 P VAM 1K Die Gouge E

1923 D VAM 1V Die Gouge Below B

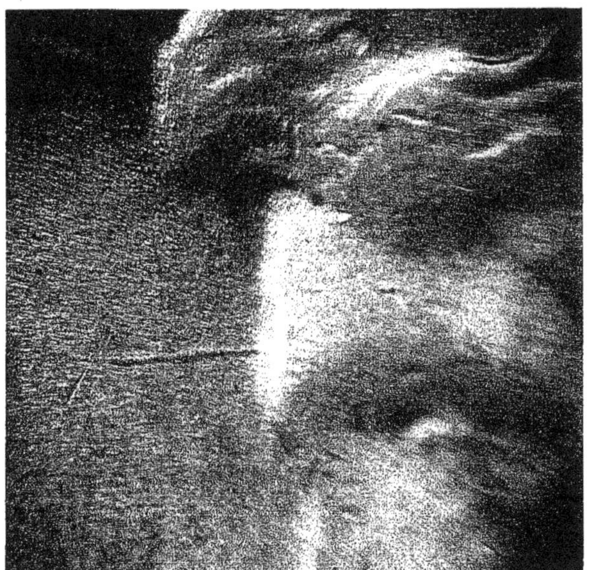

1924 P VAM 1AT Spiked Forehead

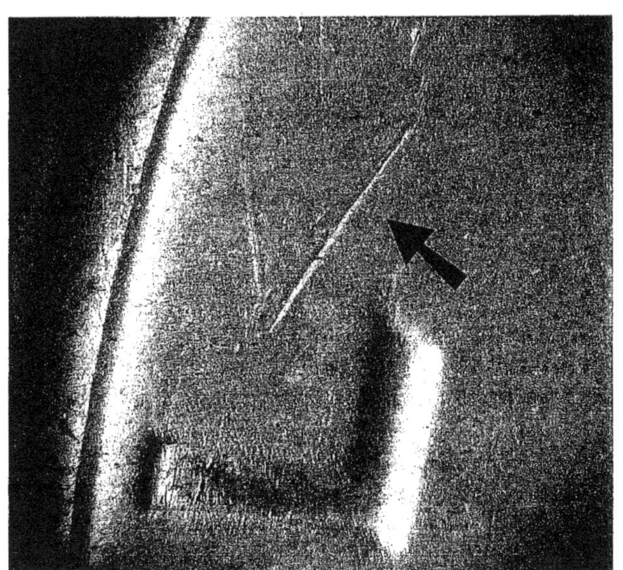

1926 D VAM 1C Die Scratch L

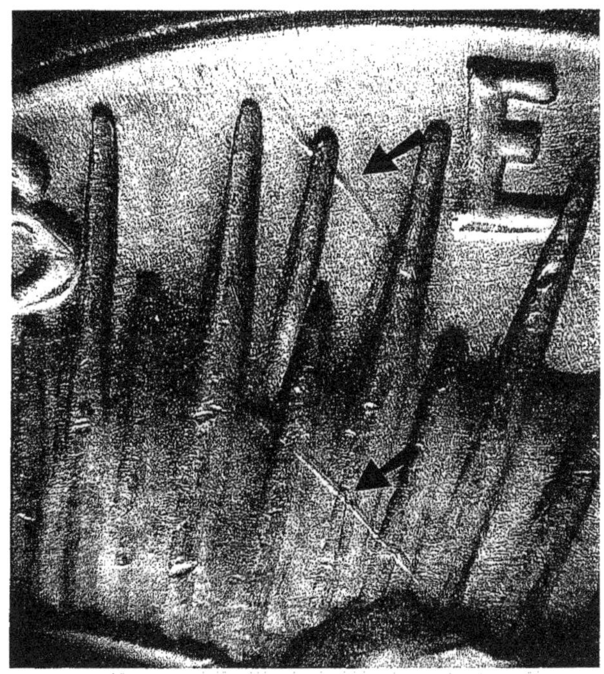

1927 D VAM 3A Die Gouges E

1922 P VAM 1BQ Die Scratch WE

Double Die Edge Contact Gouges

There are a few examples of Peace dollars obverse dies that have **two fairly closely spaced parallel** and **short die gouges**. As shown in the diagram in the chapter, **Measuring Die Rim Width And Depth**, a reverse die **tilted about 20° to 30° from the normal perpendicular or upright position** would have allowed **simultaneous contact** by the **inner and outer rim edges**. This would have produced parallel **die gouges spaced about 0.027" apart** as shown in another diagram in that later chapter. Due to the tolerances in machining the rim notch by a lathe at that time, perhaps the spacing between the inner and outer rim edges could have varied from around **0.025" to 0.030"**.

Therefore, **two parallel die gouges or scratches** on the Peace dollar obverse that have **spacings of 0.025" to 0.030"** were likely the result of a **tilted reverse die of 20° to 30° from the upright position making simultaneous contact by the inner and outer rim edges.** This is similar to the Morgan dollar obverse die making simultaneous contact with the lower revere die by the denticle spaces and the outer rim edge. Several cases are known for Morgan dollar reverse dies showing denticle impressions with an adjacent die gouge or scratch line with 0.025" separation.

Apparently the tilt angle of the contacting revere Peace dollar die with both the inner and outer die edges on the lower obverse die was a **fairly rare occurrence**. This was because a fairly substantial tilt of the reverse die was required and would only occur over a narrow tilt angle of perhaps 20° to 30°. Most reverse die contacts with the lower obverse die were likely made at a smaller tilt angle providing only one die gouge line by the **inner die edge**. The die setters were probably careful in trying to hold the upper reverse die upright for insertion into the hole in the upper triangle of the coining press.

The following are the listings and photographs of the few known double die edge contact gouges on the Peace dollar obverse die that have about the correct 0.025" to 0.030" spacing. A total of **10** double die edge contact gouges have been reported with **six** for the **Philadelphia Mint, one** for the **Denver Mint** and **three** for the **San Francisco Mint**. The most prominent example is the **1922 P VAM 2N** with two heavy die gouges in the hair behind the eye as reported by **Bill Van Note in February 2000.** An unusual example is that of **1926 S VAM 1B2** reported by **David Close in 2006** with multiple thin die gouges at the top edge of the Liberty head. Some of these pairs have spacings of 0.025". Other examples of 1923 D VAM 1CB, 1924 P VAM 1BE and 1925 VAMs 1Q & 1AG, and show several sets of parallel die scratches in the same area with 0.025" to 0.030" spacing where the inner and outer rim edges were simultaneously brushed or made light contact several times with the lower obverse dies.

1922 P VAMs 1E/2L, 2N, 2AM
1923 D VAM 1CB
1923 S VAM 1AZ
1924 P VAM 1BE
1925 P VAMs 1Q, 1AG
1926 S VAMs 1B2, 1I1

1922 P VAM 2N Double Die Gouges Hair

1922 P VAM 1E/2L Double Die Gouges Between IB

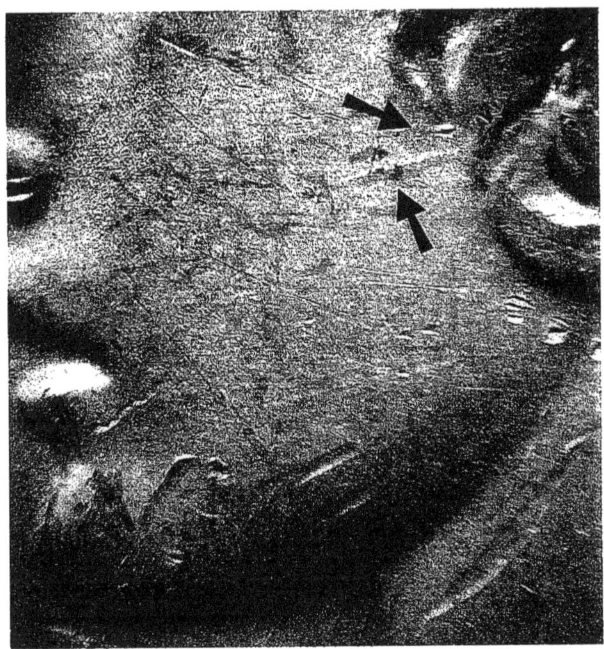
1922 P VAM 2AM Double Die Gouges Back of Cheek

1923 D VAM 1CB Double Die Scratches Rear Ray

1923 S VAM 1AZ Double Die Scratches Last Ray

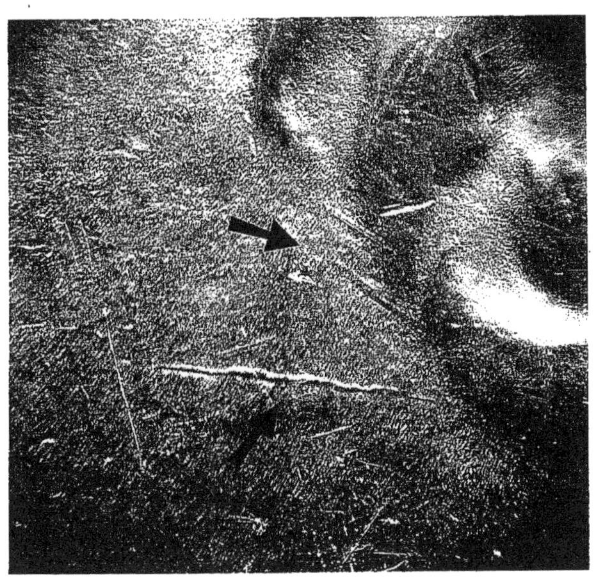
1924 P VAM 1BE Double Die Scratches Face

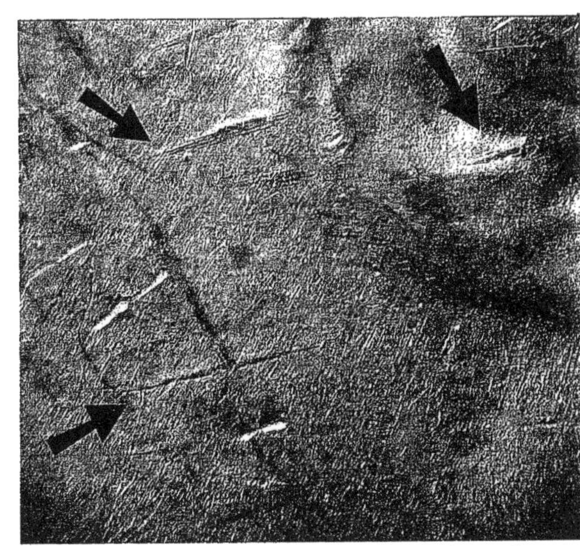
1925 P VAM 1Q Double Die Gouges Cheek

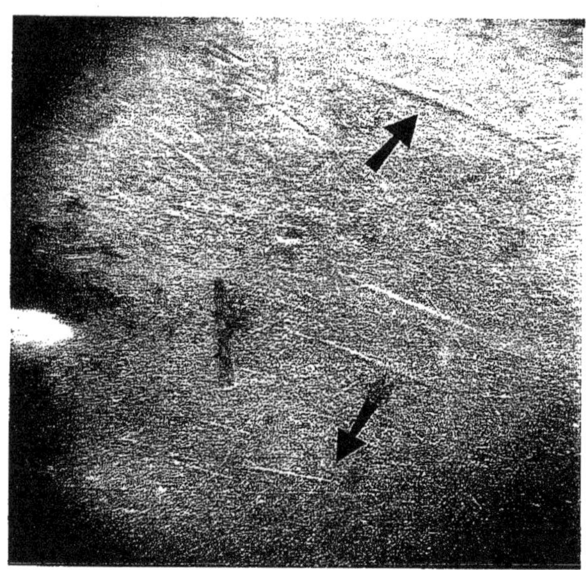
1925 P VAM 1AG Double Die Scratches Face

1926 S VAM 1B2 Double Die Gouges Below R

1926 S VAM 1I1 Double Die Scratches

Die Edge Contact Gouges, Reverse

There are a number of Peace dollar reverse dies that show **single slightly curved lines** with **tapered ends** and medium length. These look **very similar** to the **die edge contact gouges** on the **obverse** as discussed and illustrated in the previous section, **Die Edge Contact, Obverse**. They have basically the **same cause** as those gouges on the obverse. Only in this case it was due to the obverse inner rim edge contacting or brushing against the upper reverse die.

It was likely that the die setter sometimes removed or installed the lower obverse die while the upper reverse die was still in the coining press. Instances could have occurred that as the lower obverse die was switched in or out of the coining press, it was accidently contacted or brushed against the exposed upper reverse die face. The collar surrounding the lower die would have had to been removed to gain access to the lower die. Since the upper **reverse die face was open and exposed**, die gouges and scratches could have **occurred anywhere on the reverse die face**.

Only **19 possible die edge contact gouges** on the upper reverse dies have been reported so far, considerably less than the 61 for the equivalent die edge gouges on the lower obverse dies. An early reporting of die edge gouge on the reverse die was by **David Close** in **May 2001** for the **1923 D VAM 1G.** The most are again for the **Philadelphia Mint** of **10, seven** for the **San Francisco Mint** and only **two** for the **Denver Mint**. Some example die edge contact gouges and scratches on the Peace dollar reverse dies are shown in the accompanying photographs. **Appendix C, Die Edge Gouges On Reverse**, shows the photographs of all the currently reported die edge gouges and scratches on the reverse.

1922 P VAMs 2AE, 2BW
1922 D VAM 13B
1922 S VAMs 1AD, 2M, 2N1/2AG, 2AB
1923 P VAMs 1Q, 1AJ, 1BI
1923 D VAM 1G
1923 S VAM 1BI
1925 P VAMs 1P, 17A
1925 S VAM 1C
1935 P VAMs 1A, 1B, 1C
1935 S VAM 5A

1922 P VAM 2AE Die Gouge DOLL

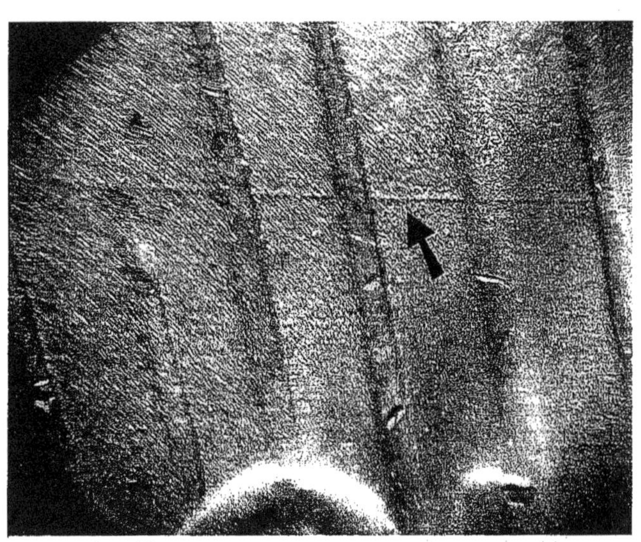

1922 P VAM 2BW Die Scratch Above DOL

1922 S VAM 2M Die Gouge Wing

1922 S VAM 2AB Die Gouge Below AR

1923 D VAM 1G Die Gouge Rays

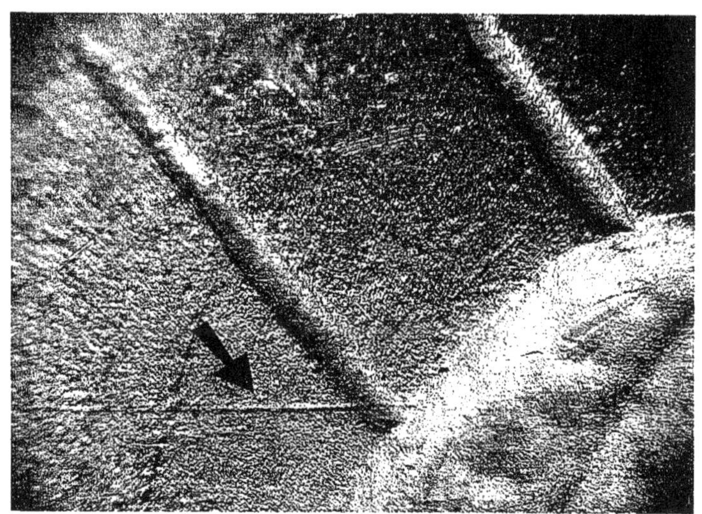

1925 P VAM 1P Die Scratch Wing

1935 P VAM 1A Die Scratch Olive Leaves

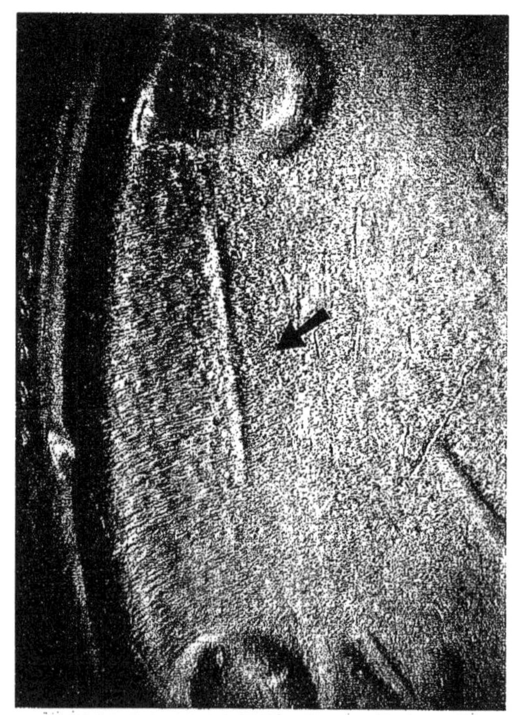

1925 S VAM 1C Die Gouge Below U

Die Gouges And Scratches Without Specific Cause

This section treats **die gouges and scratches that don't have a <u>ready explanation</u> for their cause**. Separate previous sections covered the **specific causes** of die gouge and scratches found on Peace dollars, namely:

- Feed Finger Die Gouges
- Die Edge Gouges
- Beveled Field From Feed Fingers
- 1923 D Gouges on Obverse

Scratches are **<u>thin raised lines</u>** on coins **visible to the naked eye** and **gouges** are **<u>wider and thicker bars</u>**. They range greatly in size and length. Only those **readily visible to the naked eye** are listed as die varieties. Fine polishing lines that aren't visible to the naked eye can sometimes be useful as die markers.

Possible Other Causes of Die Gouges

Besides the previously mentioned causes of some gouges and scratches on the Peace dollar dies, there are several other possible causes. These can't be related to specific reported die gouges varieties at the present time. Gouges and scratches can occur on working dies before they were first used in the coining presses thru **accidental damage during transit** from the Philadelphia Mint where they were produced and at the mints as they were moved around. They can also be damaged during the **removal of the dies to be repaired and polished** after receiving die clash marks or cracks and in **transit and storage** between multiple installations in the coining presses as die pairs were changed and mixed up. Generally, these unexplained die gouges are **wide bars, curved gouges, striated gouges**, and **not the vertical bars** on the lower obverse.

Reported Unexplained Die Gouges

Over **56 unexplained die gouges and scratches** are currently listed with their number being about evenly divided between the obverse ane reverse dies. There are **34** for the **Philadelphia Mint, 18** for the **San Francisco Mint** and **four** for the **Denver Mint**.

The following lists the die gouges and scratches die varieties without specific causes and some example photographs are shown of the more spectacular ones. **Appendix D, Unexplained Die Gouges And Scratches** shows the photographs of all the currently reported unexplained die varieties. The **first** unexplained die gouge was **reported** by **Jeff Oxman in April 1999** for the **1923 VAM 1I** with striated gouge thru E. The next two were by **David Close in December 1999** for a wide gouge thru the **left S in STATES** of **1923 D VAM 1A and a 1922 S VAM 2A** with short gouge below the tail feathers **by Bill Van Note in December 1999.**

The **1922 P VAM 2CN** has an **extra ray below the tail feather**. There is a wide **'flaming ray'** die gouge above ONE for the **1922 S VAM 2C**. Strange **X die scratches** are below the eagle's claw for the **1923 P VAM 1AC1.** A **very wide** die gouge shows behind the eagle's neck for the **1923 P VAM 1BC**. An interesting **striated wide** die gouge shows at the back of the tiara band for the **1923 D VAM 1AO1.** A very **wide 'comet'** die gouge shows below R in LIBERTY on the **1926 S VAM 2A.** A similar die **gouge below R** also shows for the **1927 S VAM 1I.**

1921 Peace VAMs 1B, 1K
1922 P VAMs 1J, 1M, 1S, 2O, 2P2, 2Q, 2AD, 2AU, 2BM, 2BP, 2BV, 2CB, 2CG, 2CH, 2CN, 2DH, 3
1922 D VAMs 1AA, 8
1922 S VAMs 2A, 2C1, 2D/2J1, 2E, 2K, 2U
1923 P VAMs 1I, 1T, 1AC1, 1AK, 1BC, 1BE, 1BL, 11
1923 D VAMs 1A, 1AO1
1923 S VAMs 1H, 1V, 1AD3, 1AQ1, 1BK

1924 P VAMs 1J, 1AP, 1AR
1924 S VAMs 1H, 1J, 3
1925 P VAM 1AI
1925 S VAM 1F
1926 S VAMs 1Q, 2A
1927 S VAM 1I
1934 P VAM 1A, 1D, 1F

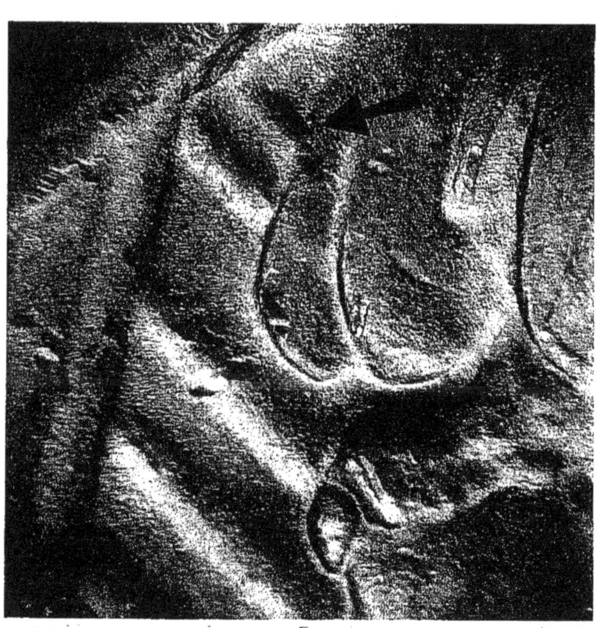

1922 P VAM 2CN Extra Ray Below Tail Feathers

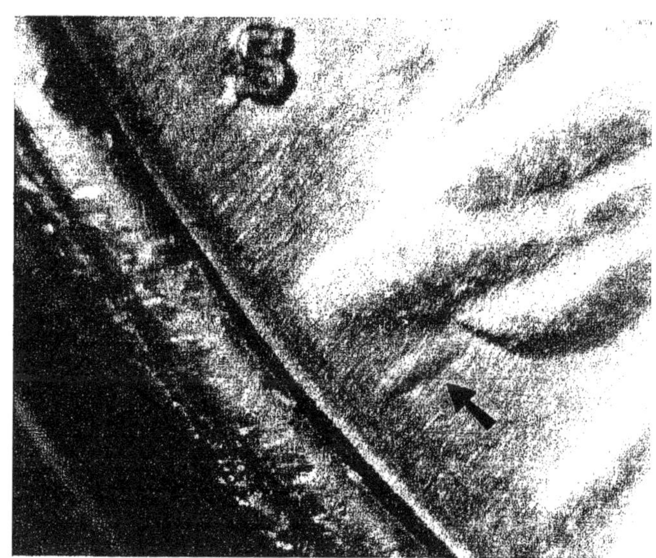

1922 S VAM 2A Spiked Tail Feathers

1922 S VAM 2C Flaming Ray Die Gouge

1923 P VAM 1I Die Gouge E

1923 P VAM 1AC1 X Die Scratches

1923 P VAM 1BC Die Gouge Above Eagle's Neck

1923 D VAM 1A Die Gouge Thru S

1923 D VAM 1AO1 Die Gouges Tiara Band

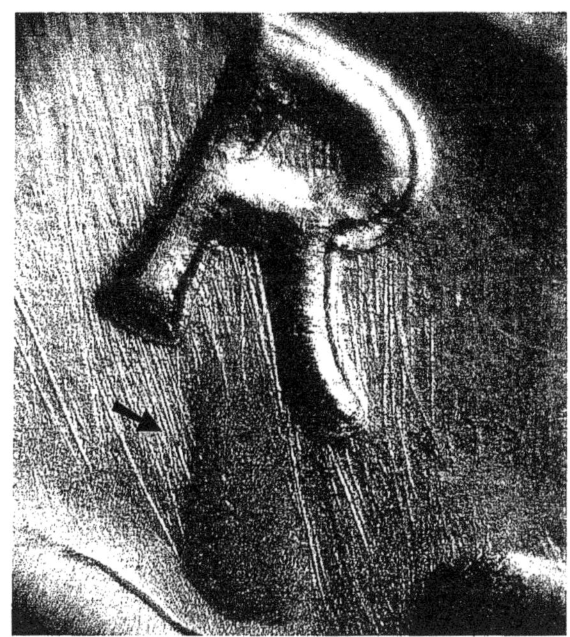

1926 S VAM 2A Comet Die Gouge R

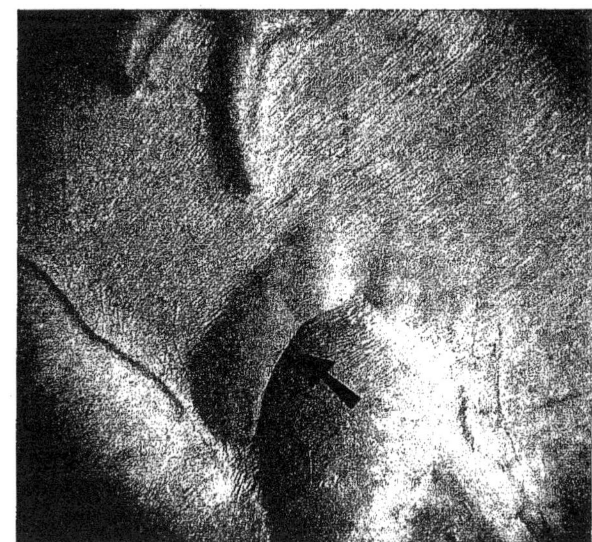

1927 S VAM 1I Die Gouges Hair Bun

1923 D Special Cases of Two Obverses Die Gouges

Two die variety listings for the 1923 D Peace dollar were reported in 2010 and early 2011 that an have **amazing number of die gouges and scratches on the obverse die**. They are the most **extensive** and **longest** ones on the Peace dollars. Some of the gouges are so long that they extend from the left rim over all across the Liberty head face! Why coins were struck with such obvious die gouges on the obverse die is a mystery. Likely the dies were only briefly used before they were pulled and polished or retired. The coins must be rare because they were only recently reported.

1923 D VAM 1BS Hooked Liberty Lip

This gouged obverse die has been dubbed the **'Hooked Liberty Lip'** by the discoverer, **Jason Henrichsen,** who reported it in **June 2010.** It has a **long horizontal heavy die gouge from the rim** over to the **Liberty head upper lip** and **connecting double lines bent upwards behind the lip,** like a hook. A **second long horizontal die scratch** with double lines extends **from the rim** above the first gouge **over to the nose, across the cheek and down to the rear jaw-neck junction**. A **third single line die scratch** is from the **rim below L over thru the eye to the hair edge**. The **fourth die scratch** goes from the **jaw-neck junction into the hair and makes a sharp turn upwards and then diagonally left in the hair**. There are also heavy die file lines at the rim from IN to 1.

Such long prominent die gouges and scratches are **unprecedented** on these two Peace dollar obverses because they are so obvious. There is nothing quite this severe of numerous long die gouges on the pre-1921 obverse for the Morgan dollar.

1923 D VAM 1BK Chin Bar

This **spectacular** die gouges on the obverse has a more complicated reporting history. It culminated with **Brian Raines** reporting in **February 2011** of a coin with an obverse die that had even **more extensive die scratches and gouges all over the Liberty head face than** the previously reported **1923 D VAM 1BS**. The **VAM 1BK was first reported in January 2010 by David Close** with a **broad vertical die gouge from the Liberty head chin** down to the top right D in GOD. Hence the moniker **'Chin Bar'**. In early February 2011, David Close sent a 1923 D along with the original VAM 1BK discovery coin showing that the new coin had a **die gouge between T & Y in LIBERTY** along with a weakened chin bar gouge. This die state was assigned **VAM 1BK2.**

The coin that Brian Raines sent in mid-February 2011 was a different die state than those of David Close. It had **many additional obverse die gouges and scratches plus the chin bar gouge** and was assigned **VAM 1BK3.** There were **gouges at RVST going above and thru the rear hair strands,** all **around LI in LIBERTY, over the top of 3** and **many light scratches going from the left rim over across the Liberty head face**. These scratches and gouges were fairly widely spaced. They are not like fine very close die file or polishing lines, vertical gouges at the lower obverse from feed fingers or the usual shorter straight or slightly curved die edge impact or grazing blow.

How Created

Such **widely spaced, long and numerous die gouges and scratches** on a Peace dollar are **unique** to these two 1923 D VAMs 1BK3 and 1BS. Something **different** must have happened to the dies to cause the unusually long and widely spaced gouges and scratches.

The Peace dollar working dies were in a **hardened state** when they left the Philadelphia Mint to be shipped to the various branch mints. To produce gouges or scratches on the die face would require contact or scraping by a special hardened file, tool, special stone or another die. A hardened die file or special stone accidentally scraping across the die face could also put scratches into the die, although a stone would likely produce closely spaced parallel lines. Since these random widely spaced lines into the die face don't resemble the well known die file or polishing lines, their deliberate creation by a die file, stone or tool **can be ruled out**.

The gouges were likely made into the die face by the **accidental scraping of the edge of another die.** Perhaps these two dies were accidentally **jostled together face-to-face while being carried in a box** or **in transit** to the Denver Mint instead of the normal upright position. A hardened die file or special stone accidentally scraping across the die face could also put scratches into the die, although a stone would likely produce closely spaced parallel lines. The **many localized scratches at L** on VAM 1BK3 is intriguing because of their **<u>intense concentration,</u>** like something sharp, such as a die edge, was jostled at the location **many times**.

1923 D VAM 1BS Die Scratch in Hair

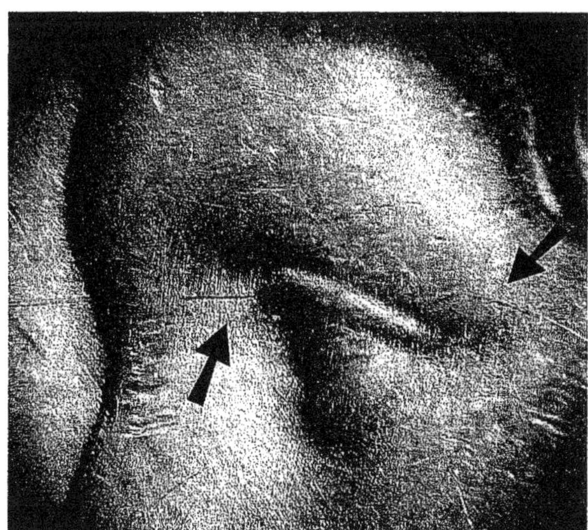

1923 D VAM 1BS Die Scratch Eye

1923 D VAM 1BS Hooked Liberty Lip Die Gouge

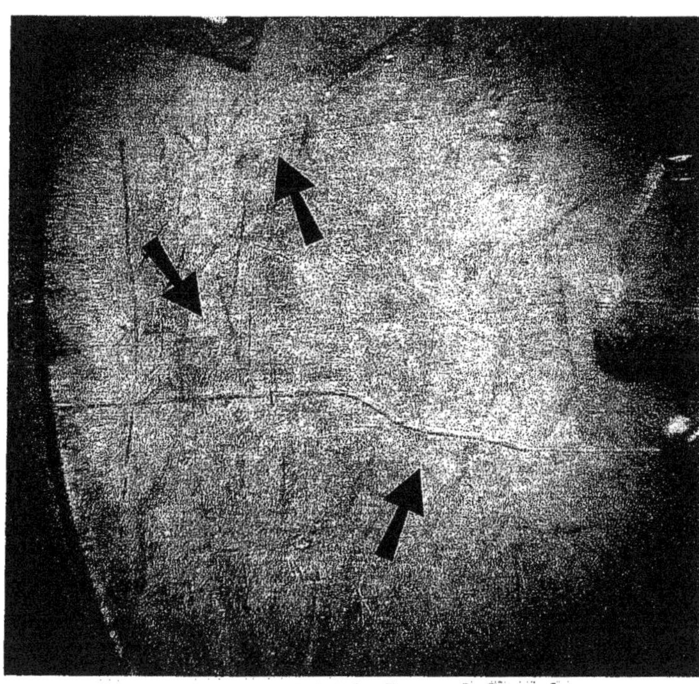

1923 D VAM 1BS Die Gouge & Scratch

1923 D VAM 1BK Die Gouge Chin

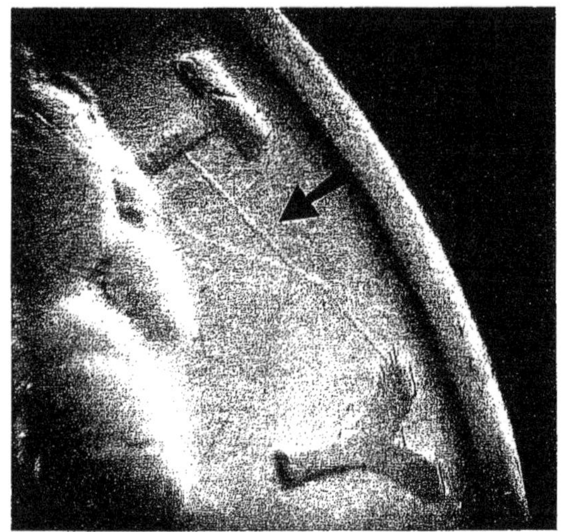

1923 D VAM 1BK2 Die Gouge TY

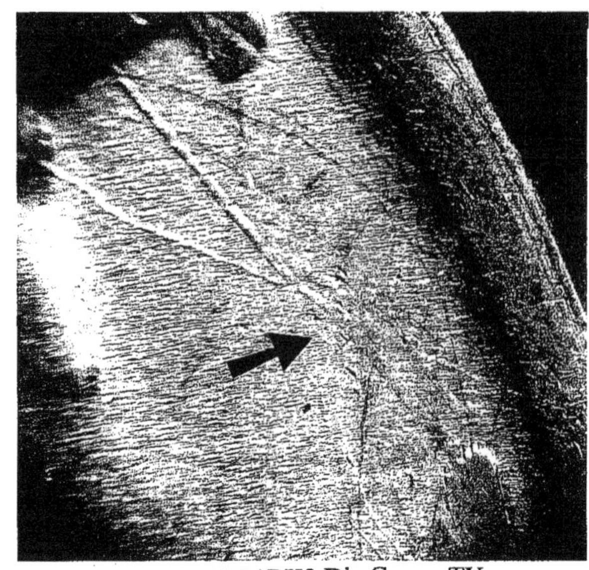

1923 D VAM 1BK3 Die Gouge TY

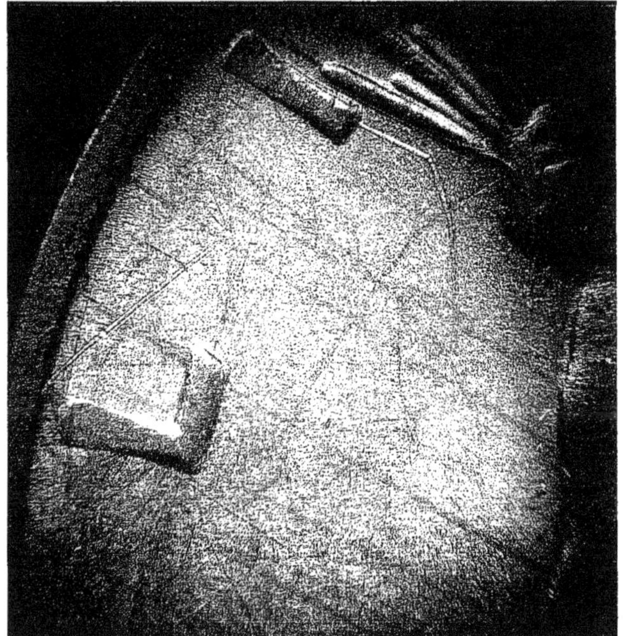

1923 D VAM 1BK3 Die Gouges/Scratches LI

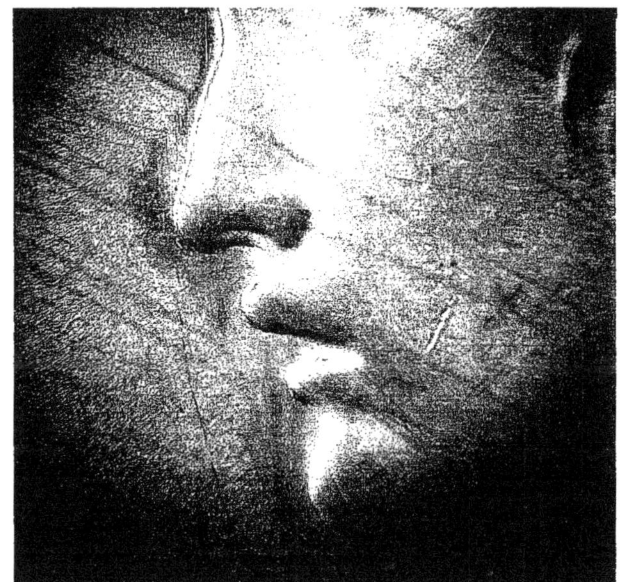

1923 D VAM 1BK3 Die Gouges/Scratches Face

1923 D VAM 1BK3 Die Gouges/Scratches L

1923 D VAM 1BK3 Die Gouges/Scratches RVST

MEASURING DIE RIM WIDTH AND DEPTH

In order to determine if certain double die scratches on the obverse of the Peace dollars are due to both the **inner and outer edges of the rim notch**, the **spacing between the two rim edges** needs to be known. Unfortunately, there were no available Peace dollar dies to check the spacing. The only things available were photographs of Morgan dollar dies of 1878 and 1884 and Ike dollar dies of 1977 plus coins of Morgan, Peace and Ike dollars. The photograph of the 1884 Morgan obverse die was at an angle and not very sharp, which made it unusable for this study.

Morgan Dollar Die

The photograph of a canceled 1878 CC reverse Morgan die was a side profile and allowed fairly accurate dimensions to be obtained, except for the rim notch. However, measurements of Morgan dollar coins were made using a mini-scale tool for microscopes that has a scale with 0.005" divisions that allowed interpretation to about 0.002". This tool is shown in the accompanying photographs. The average rim width was about 0.025" from a full outside edge to the beginning of the denticles. Thickness of the rim and of the field next to the denticles was measured with calipers and micrometer which gave a depth of about 0.010".

Ike Dollar Dies

Of course the Peace dollars do not have denticles and are a solid raised rim similar to the Ike dollar. Some accompanying photographs of 1977 Ike dollar dies show the rim notch like the Peace dollar. The body of the Ike dollar dies are not as wide as the Morgan dollar die, perhaps to reduce the amount of steel needed for each die. Measurement of the Ike dollar coin rims was somewhat difficult because they were **rounded due to the nickel outer layer** of the clad coins was much **<u>harder</u>** than the silver in the Morgan and Peace dollar coins and **didn't fully strike up.** But they typically had a width of about 0.025" from estimates of their full widths.

Peace Dollar Dies

The overall Peace dollar die shape likely was **<u>similar</u>** to the Morgan dollar dies since only 17 years had elapsed from the regular Morgan dollar production end in 1904 and the Peace dollar production in 1921. Besides, the Morgan dollars and Peace dollars were **struck in the same year** in 1921. Also, the Ike dollar was struck some 50 years later. So the Peace dollar dies were likely of the Morgan dollar shape with a rim notch similar to the Ike dollar dies but no denticles.

Measuring Peace Dollar Coin Rims

Measurements were made of several different years of Peace dollar coins that had visible finning lines at the rim. Finning is a raised thin ridge beyond the normal flat rim top caused by planchet metal forced up between the die shoulder and collar. The **sharp line at the finning and rim junction** is an **accurate indication of the die rim notch outside edge**. The accompanying photographs thru a 30X stereo microscope shows the mini-scale digit 1 at the finning line for several Peace dollar dates of 1921, 1922 P, 1922 D and 1924 P. Several photographs for this scale are at the edge of a full rim for the 1921 reverse, 1924 P reverse and 1934 D obverse and reverse. The results show a rim width of **0.030" for the 1921 Peace** and **0.025" for the later Peace dollar dates**. Other Peace dollar dates were also measured with the same results.

The height of the rim notch was obtained by measuring the full thickness of the rim and adjacent coin field on a number of Peace dollar coins using a caliper and micrometer. The average field thickness was subtracted from the average rim thickness and divided in half to obtain the single obverse or reverse die rim notch height. **This was a consistent 0.010".**

Distance Between Rim Edges

The distance between the inside and outside rim edges was then obtained mathematically using the 0.025" width and 0.010" height of the die edge notch. The distance between the rim edges was **about 0.027"** which is the **distance between the two die scratches** when **both edges of the upper reverse die contacted the lower obverse die.**

Correspondence from the Philadelphia Mint Die Manufacturing Division in 1979 stated that the dimension tolerances for the working die length was +/- one thousand and diameters was +/- two tenths of a thousand. The tolerances for the Peace dollar dies some 50 years earlier was likely not as small. Even with a tolerance of one thousand on the rim notch dimensions, the gap distance between the inner and outer rim edges wouldn't vary much over +/- one thousand of the nominal 0.027". A **double die scratch or gouge spacing** of **0.025" to 0.030"** should cover any scratches thought to be due to the die **inner and outer rim edges** contacting the die field simultaneously.

Die Edge Contact Angle

The remaining question of double die edge contact is the **angle for contact a reasonable one** during the die installation process in the coining presses. The accompanying sketch shows the rim notch contact angle on the flat field for the single line of the inside edge, single line of the outside edge and the angle for the double lines contact for both inside and outside edges. The angle from the normal perpendicular upright position for **double edge contact is about 22°.** This perhaps may vary from about 20° to 25° with the die edge dimension tolerances, depth of edge contact and uneven depth of inner and outer edge contact.

This tilting of the upper reverse die during it's installation in the coining press would seem to be **reasonable variance** in the handling of the die by the die setter.

Conclusion

The conclusion is that **parallel die scratches** on a die with **spacing of around 0.025" to 0.030"** were likely made by **simultaneous contact** of the **inner and outer edges of the rim notch** of the Peace dollar die during installation or removal in the coining presses. Only a **tilt of about 22°** from the **upright position** would result in **simultaneous contact** of the **inner and outer die rim edges.** This is similar to the Morgan dollar cases of denticle impressions with the die edge scratch below with spacing of about 0.025". **Most die edge scratches** were **likely made** by the **inner rim die edge** with small tilts of the reverse die.

These double die scratches can be measured directly on a coin using a mini-scale and 10X loupe or 10X to 20X stereo microscope. The alternative is to use a 10X loupe to mark the distance of a Peace dollar rim width of 0.025" on the edge of a piece of paper. The marked edge of the paper can then be used to determine if the double scratch line spacing is about the same of 0.027", again using a 10X loupe.

Ike Dollar Die Edge, 1977

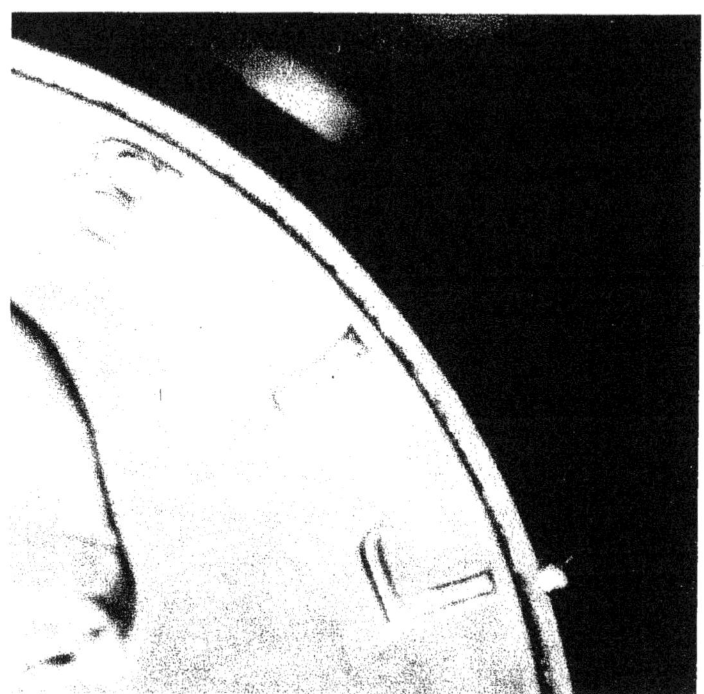
Ike Dollar Die Edges

Canceled 1878 CC Dollar Die 1

Ike Dollar Die Shape

Mini-scale for Microscopes

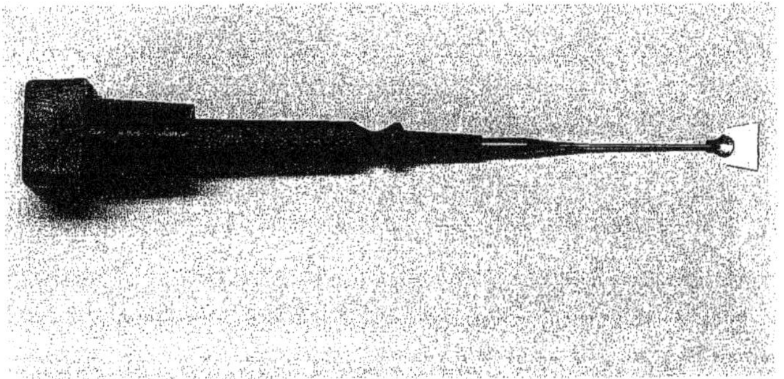
Mini-scale Tool for Microscopes

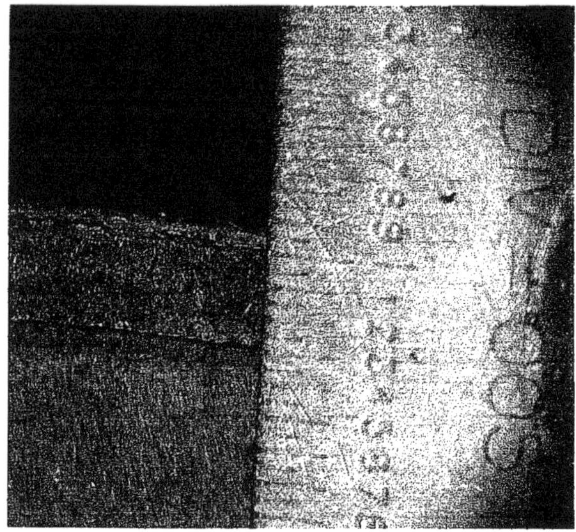
1921 Peace Obv 0.030" Rim Width To Finning Line

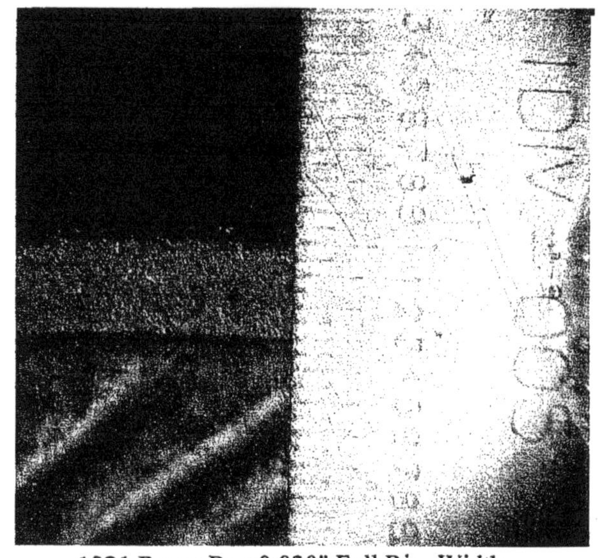
1921 Peace Rev 0.030" Full Rim Width

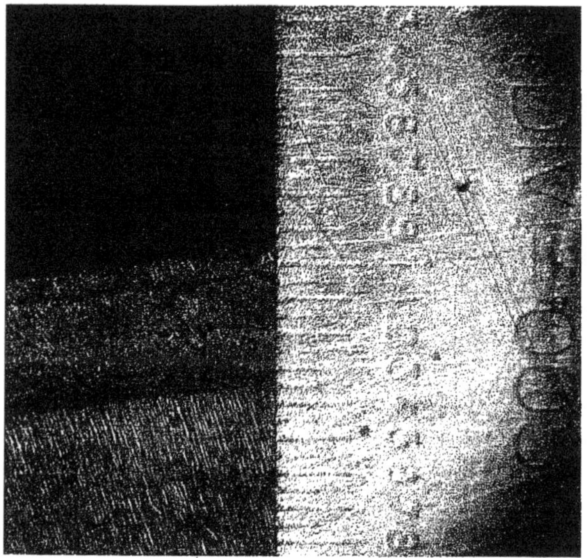
1922 P Obv 0.030" Rim Width To Finning Line

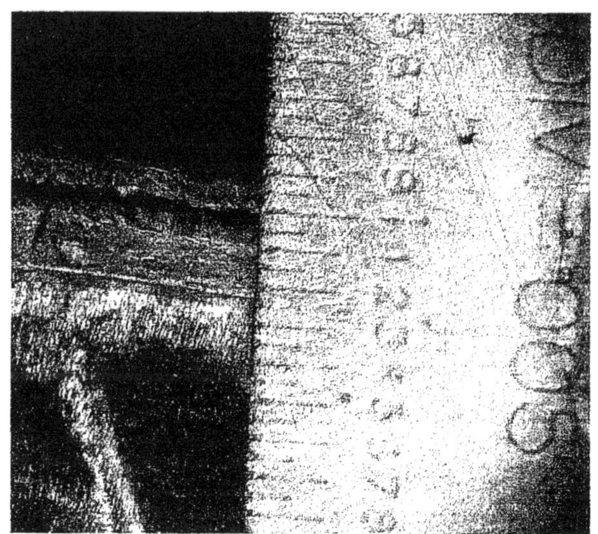
1922 P B2 Rev 0.025" Rim Width To Finning Line

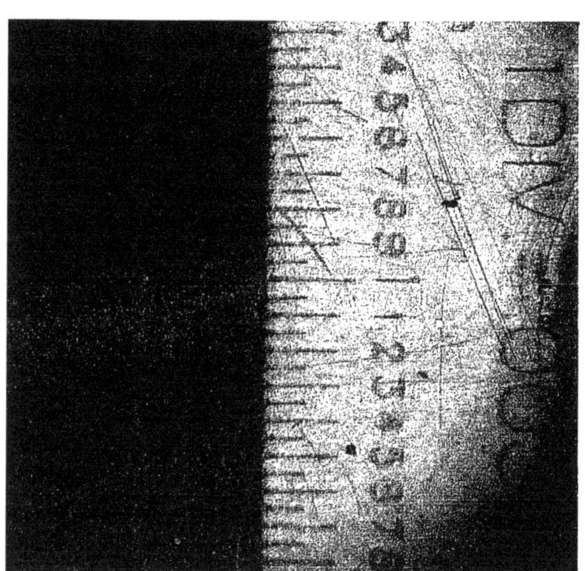
1922 D Obv 0.025" Rim Width To Finning Line

1922 D B2 Rev 0.025" Rim Width To Finning Line

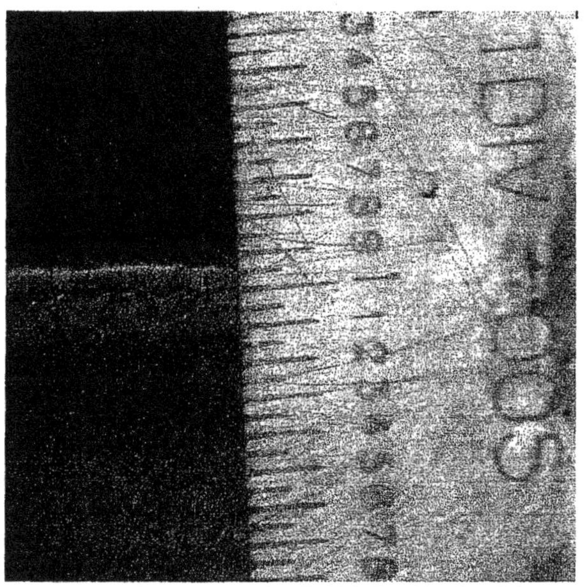

1924 P Obv 0.025" Rim Width To Finning Line

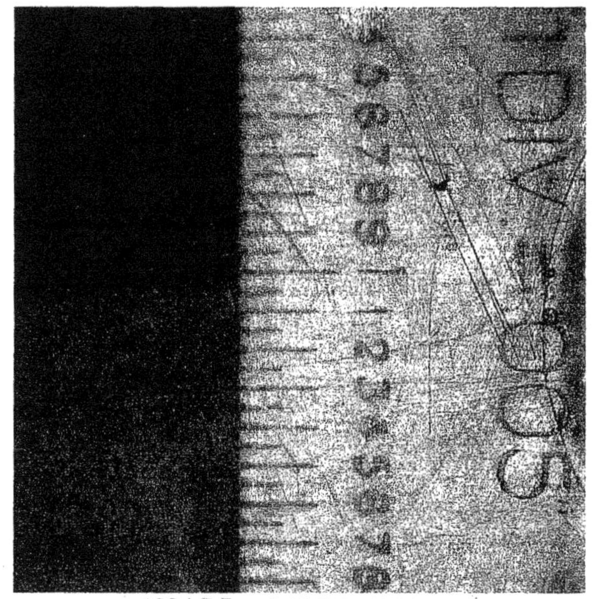

1924 P Rev 0.025" Full Rim

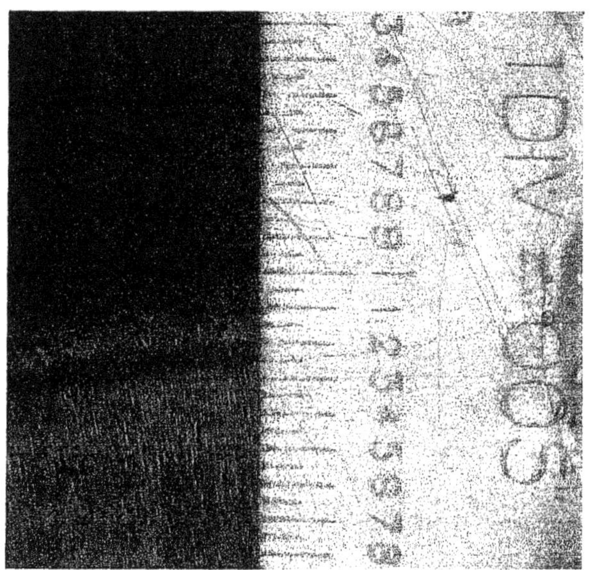

1934 D Obv 0.025" Full Rim

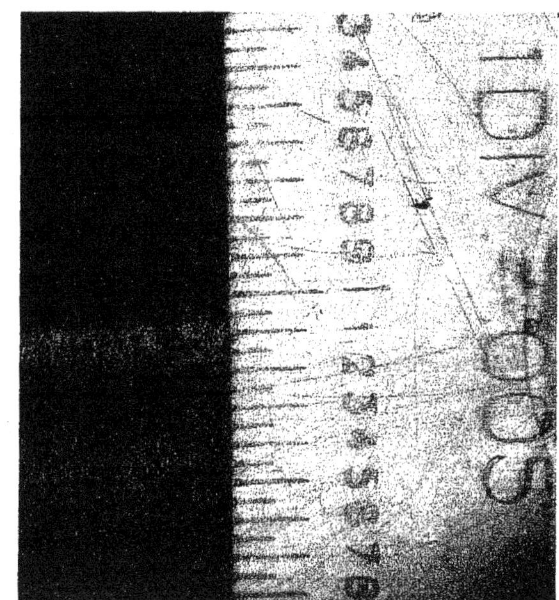

1934 D Rev 0.025" Full Rim

X
0.010
0.025

$$X = \sqrt{0.025^2 + 0.010^2} = 0.0269$$

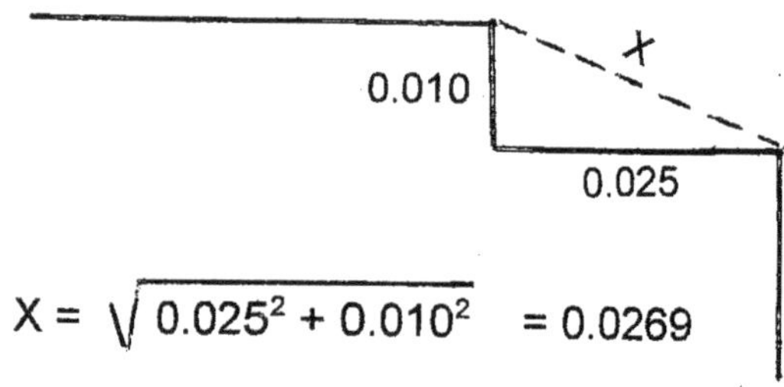

Edge Rim Dimensions

Dimensions are in inches
0.025
Rim Notch
0.010
1.50
1.45
0.25
0.31
2.0
1.43
1.75

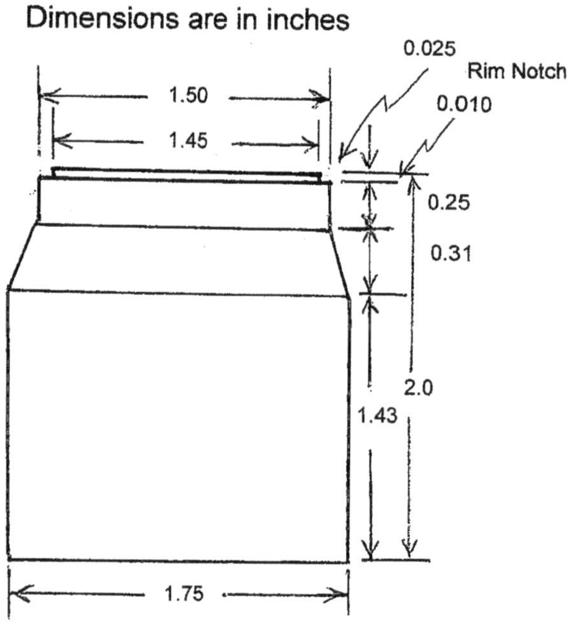

Morgan Dollar Die Dimensions
(Likely Also Peace Dollar Dies)

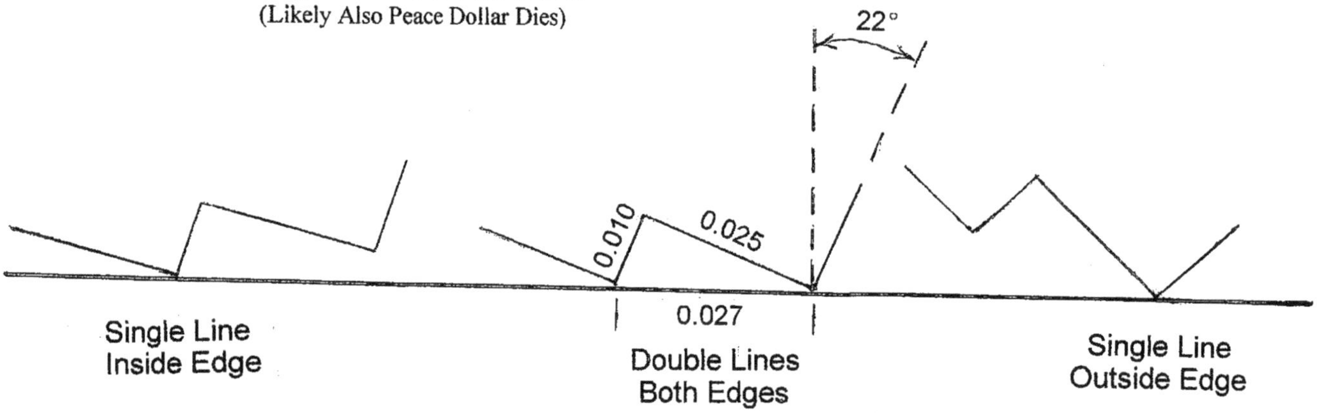

22°
0.010
0.025
0.027
Single Line
Inside Edge
Double Lines
Both Edges
Single Line
Outside Edge

Possible Die Edge Contacts

TOP 30 PEACE DOLLAR GOUGES

The following are some selected die gouges as the **Top 30 Peace Dollar** die gouges. There are a few chosen from each of the seven die gouge cause categories discussed in this document: Feed Fingers, Beveled Fields, Die Edge Obverse, Double Die Edge Obverse, Die Edge Reverse, Unexplained, and Two 1923 D. Those selected for the Top 30 were primarily based on their **extent, severity** and **visible location**. It was **difficult to pare down** the selection to just 30 out of the total currently listed of 269 gouges and scratches. The reader undoubtedly has other die gouge favorites.

There are eight die gouge varieties automatically included in this Top 30 Peace dollar gouges listing because they are in the documents of *The Official Guide To The Top 50 Peace Dollar Varieties* by Jeff Oxman and Dr. David Close, 2002, and *The Elite 30 Peace Dollar VAMs* by Dr. David Close and C. Ash Harrison, 2013. The **Top 50** die gouges includes 1922 P VAM 1A, 2F, 1923 P VAM 1F, 1924 P VAM 1A, 1925 P VAM 1A. The 1926 S VAM 4 isn't included although it was mentioned as possible gouge from a tool. Another possible cause may be a die flaw that caused a break. Because of unclear cause, it is not currently included as a clear die gouge, such as a long raised line on a coin. The **Elite 30** die gouges includes 1922 P VAM 1E/2L, 1923 P VAM 1G and 1934 P VAM 1A.

The desirability number of stars is a **subjective number** of the author. It is primarily based on the visibility, location extent, severity and uniqueness of the die gouge. The included **Top 50** and **Elite 30** are automatically assigned five stars. Readers may have other selections for Top die gouges and their desirability. But that is part of the fun and enjoyment of collecting die varieties– each collector can choose their favorites and ones that interest them the most. Following the Top 30 Peace Dollar Die Gouges chart are photographs of each of the 30 die varieties for easy identification.

TOP 30 PEACE DOLLAR DIE GOUGES

Date	VAM Variety #	Type Gouge	Gouge Location		Desirability
1921 P	1J	Feed fingers	Rev ME		★★★★
1922 P	1A	Die edge	Rays below B	**Top 50**	★★★★★
"	1E/2L	Die edge	Rays left of B	**Elite 30**	★★★★★
"	1Q	Feed fingers	Below N-G		★★★★★
"	2F	Die edge	Rays below E	**Top 50**	★★★★
"	2N	Double die edge	Hair behind eye		★★★★★
"	2Q	Unexplained gouge	Above T		★★★★
1922 D	1F	Die edge	Thru eye		★★★★
1922 S	2C	Unexplained gouge	Flaming ray above E (rev)		★★★★★
"	2D/2J	Unexplained gouge	Thru G		★★★★
"	2U	Unexplained gouge	Below WE		★★★★
1923 P	1F	Feed fingers	Chin bar thru D	**Top 50**	★★★★★
"	1G	Die edge	Rays below B	**Elite 30**	★★★★★
"	1K	Die edge	Thru E of PLURIBUS		★★★★
"	1P	Die edge	R in PLURIBUS		★★★★
"	1Q	Die edge rev	Rays back eagle's claws		★★★
"	1AB	Beveled field	Rim below TRVST		★★★★
"	1AC	Unexplained gouge	X scratches below claw		★★★
"	1AS	Feed fingers	Above & below R in TRVST		★★★★
1923 D	1G	Die edge rev	Rays above OLLA		★★★★
"	1BK	Two die faces together	All over obverse		★★★★★
"	1BS	Two die faces together	Middle & left obverse		★★★★★
"	1CF	Feed fingers	Lips & chin		★★★★
1924 P	1A	Feed fingers	Bar at OD	**Top 50**	★★★★★
1925 P	1A	Die edge	Rays below E	**Top 50**	★★★★★
1925 S	1C	Die edge rev	Above ONE		★★★
1926 S	2A	Unexplained gouge	Comet gouge R in PLURIBUS		★★★★★
1927 S	1I	Unexplained gouge	Gouges hair bun top		★★★★
1934 P	1A	Unexplained gouge	19 to G	**Elite 30**	★★★★★
1935 P	1A	Die edge rev	3 at olive leaves, above R, rt of eagle's shoulder		★★★★

1921 Peace VAM 1J Feed Fingers Die Gouge ME

1922 P VAM 1A Die Edge Gouge Rays

1922 P VAM 1E/2L Die Edge Gouge IB

1922 P VAM 1Q Feed Fingers Die Gouge NG

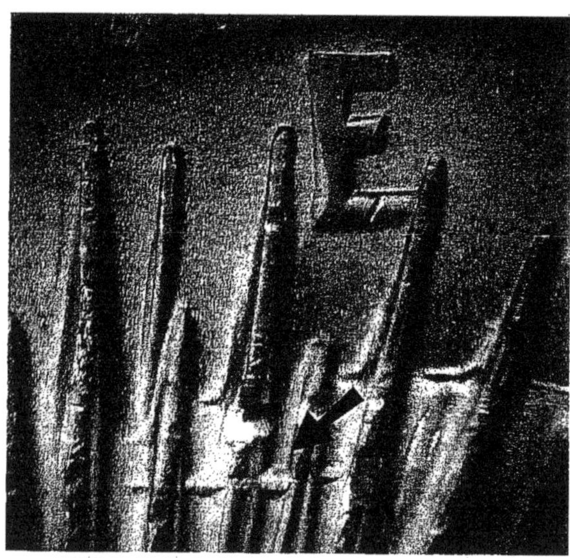
1922 P VAM 2F Die Edge Gouge Below E

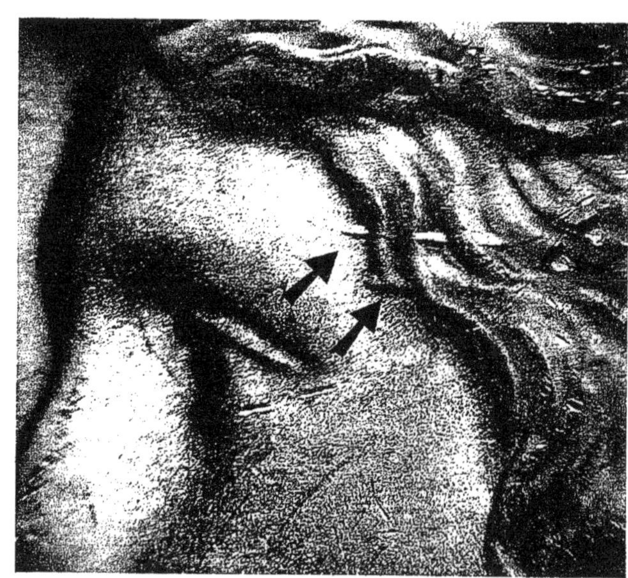
1922 P VAM 2N Double Die Edge Gouges

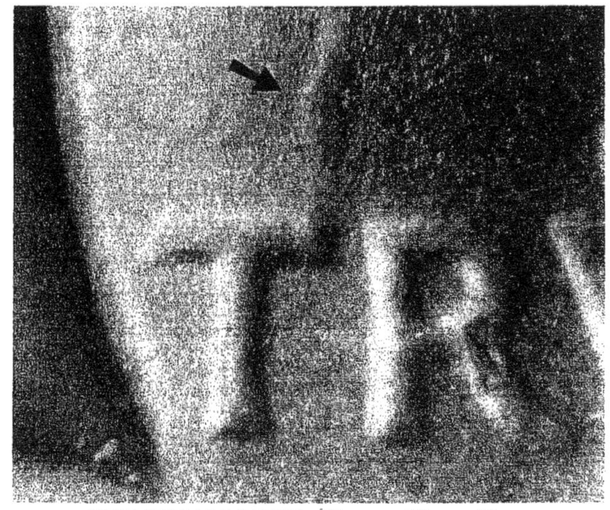
1922 P VAM 2Q Die Gouge Above T

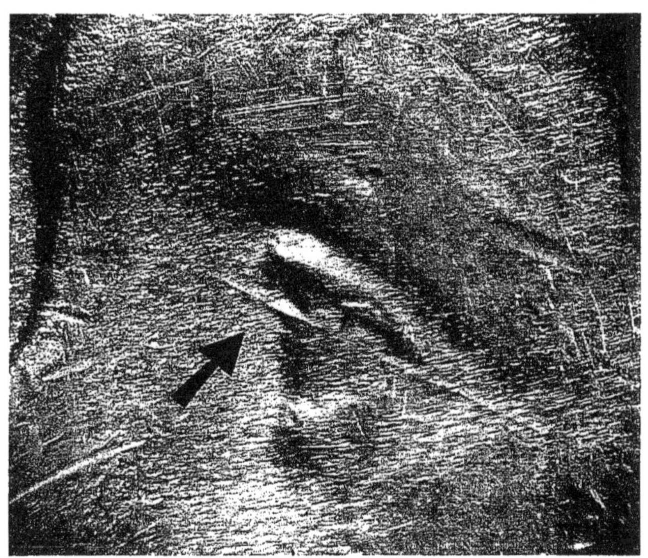
1922 D VAM 1F Die Edge Spiked Eye

1922 S VAM 2C Flaming Ray Die Gouge Above ONE

1922 S VAM 2D/2J Die Gouge G

1922 S VAM 2U Die Gouge Below WE

1923 P VAM 1F Chin Bar Feed Fingers Gouge

1923 VAM 1G Die Edge Gouge Below B

1923 P VAM 1P Die Edge Gouge R

1923 P VAM 1AB Beveled Field

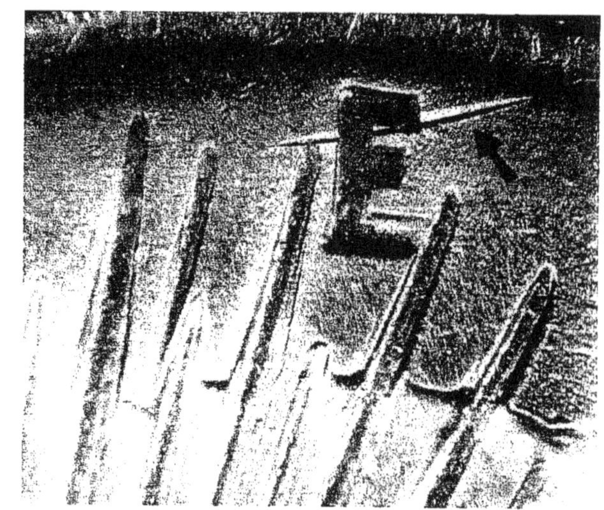

1923 P VAM 1K Die Edge Gouge E

1923 P VAM 1Q Die Edge Gouge Rays Below Tail

1923 P VAM 1AC X Die Scratches

1923 P VAM 1AS Feed Fingers Die Gouge RV

1923 D VAM 1G Die Edge Gouge Rays

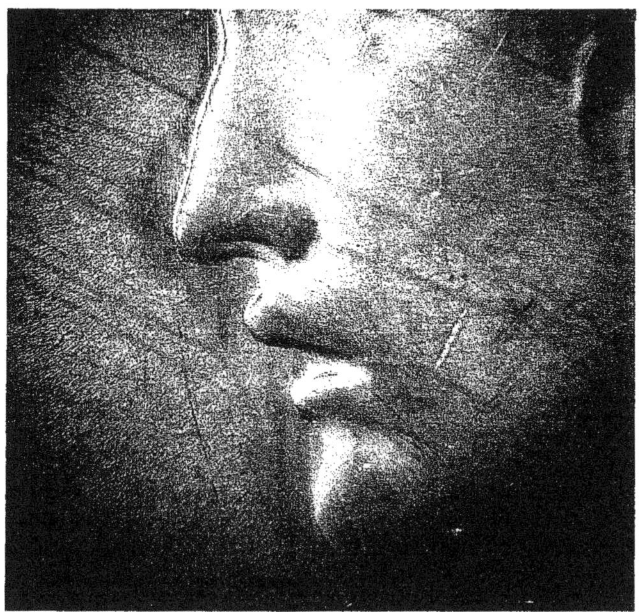
1923 D VAM 1BK Die Gouges/ Scratches Face

1923 D VAM 1BS Hooked Liberty Lip Gouge

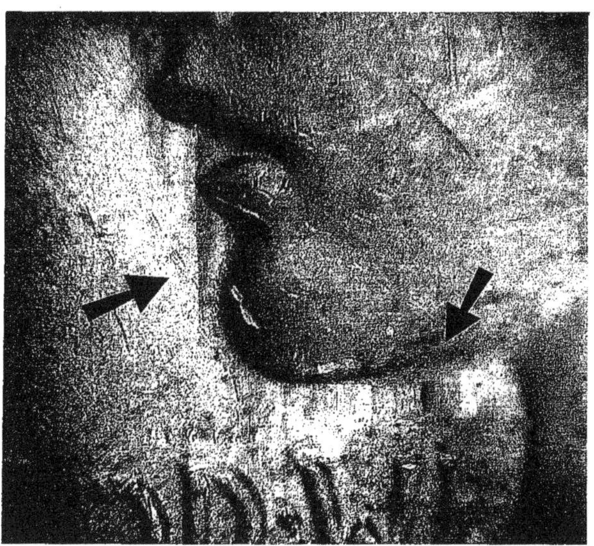
1923 D VAM 1CF Feed Fingers Gouges Lips & Jaw

1924 P VAM 1A Feed Fingers Bar D

1925 P VAM 1A Die Edge Gouge Rays

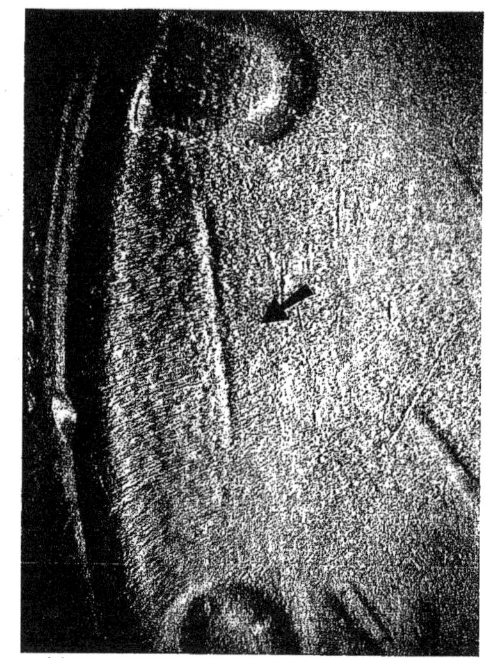
1925 S VAM 1C Die Edge Gouge U

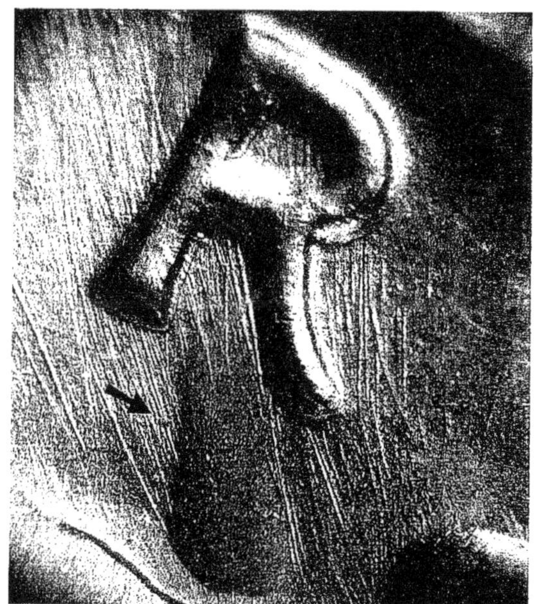
1926 S VAM 2A Comet Die Gouge

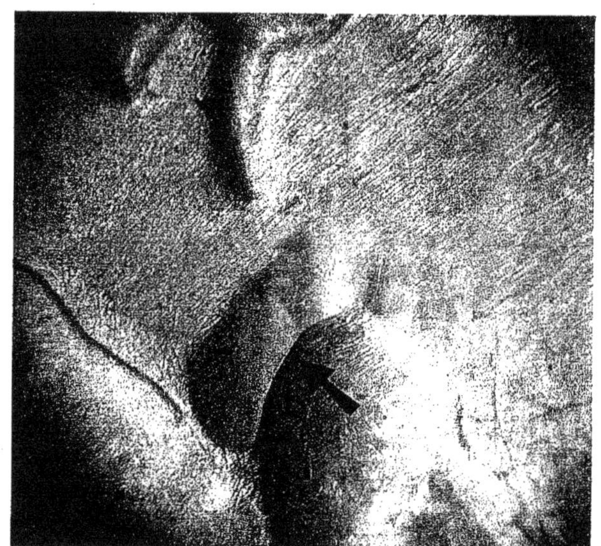
1927 S VAM 1I Die Gouges Hair Bun

1934 P VAM 1A Semi-circular Die Scratch

1935 P VAM 1A Die Edge Scratch Olive Leaves

DIE GOUGES AND SCRATCHES DESCRIPTIVE LISTINGS

This chapter contains the **descriptive listings** of all the known **VAM die gouges and scratches varieties** that have been reported for the Peace dollar series **thru August 2013.** Polishing lines and die file lines are not included.

The descriptive listings show a **summary in bold face type** on **one line** of the **die variety designation** and the **obverse** and **reverse die designations,** including the **design type** such as **II** for the obverse and $\mathbf{B^1}$ **or** $\mathbf{B^2}$ for the reverse. Specific obverse and reverse dies are given after the type designation such as **II 1, 2, 3** etc. and $\mathbf{B^2}$**a, b, c** with **numbers** for the obverse and **lower case letters** for the reverse.

Next in parenthesis is the **short descriptive die title.** At the extreme right is the **Interest Factor, I,** of 1 to 5 with 1 being normal and 5 being an outstanding high interest die variety. This is followed by the **Rarity Scale, R,** with 1 being common of tens of millions to 8 being unique or nearly unique. Each rarity number has quantities reduced by a **factor of 10** such as 2 being several millions, 3 hundreds of thousands, etc. Below are the **separate descriptions** for the **obverse and reverse die** as applicable. All Peace dollar s have an **edge reeding** count of **189.**

The listing of die varieties are generally **in the order** of when they were **reported. Die varieties** are assigned **numbers** and **sub-varieties** are given by the parent die variety number **followed by a capital letter**. In some cases, a sub-variety letter may be followed by a **number** which is a further break down into **sub-sub-variety** die states or another die.

LIST OF DIE GOUGES AND SCRATCHES VARIETIES DESCRIPTIVE LISTINGS

Reporting years, no sign **1999** and prior years
• New/revised in **Jan-Dec 2000**
✶ New/revised in **Jan-Dec 2001**
▫ New/revised in **Jan-Dec 2002**
○ New/revised in **Jan-Dec 2003**
∇ New/revised in **Jan-Dec 2004**
§ New/revised in **Jan-Dec 2005**
♯ New/revised in **Jan-Dec 2006**
¶ New/revised in **Jan 2007 thru Feb 2008**
▸ New/revised in **Feb 2008 thru Feb 2009**
✓ New/revised in **Feb– Dec 2009**
✚ New/revised in **Jan- Dec 2010**
◇ New/revised in **Jan- Dec 2011**
✗ New/revised in **Jan- Dec 2012**
♮ New revised in **Jan- Aug 2013**

1921 P (Peace)

▫1B **I 1 • Aa (Die Gouge Above ONE)** **I-2** **R-5**
Reverse Aa– Small die gouge with ovaloid dot shape just above N in ONE.

♯1E1 **I 1 • Aa (Die Gouges Reverse Left Field)** **I-2** **R-5**
Reverse Aa– Three horizontal die gouges in field near eagle's left wing.

♯1E2 **I 1 • Aa (Die Gouges Reverse Left Field, Gouge MEU)** **I-3** **R-6**
Reverse Aa– LDS with heavy vertical die gouge thru ME in AMERICA down to left tip of second U in UNUM. Gouge further left than gouge of VAM 1J. Gouge probably caused by feed fingers malfunction.

♯1 J **I 1 • Aa (Gouge ME)** **I-3** **R-5**
Reverse Aa– Heavy vertical die gouge thru ME in AMERICA down thru second U in UNUM.

♯1K1 **I 1 • Aa (Oblong Die Gouge Back of Neck)** **I-2** **R-5**
Obverse I1– Short oblong die gouge at back of neck up near hair.

♯1T **I 1 • Aa (Die Scratch RICA)** **I-2** **R-5**
Reverse Aa– Thin long die scratch from right side of R thru middle of IC over to left side of A in AMERICA.

◇1X **I 1 • Aa (Spiked Eagle, Rusted & Worn Obverse)** **I-2** **R-5**
Obverse I 1– Raised dots and splotches in left field and on Liberty head cheek and neck from worn and rusted die. Fine vertical die file lines in right field.
Reverse Aa– Short die gouge spike at edge of eagle's right wing near leg.

1922 P

✓1A(revised) **II 1 •** $\mathbf{B^1}$**a (Die Gouge in Rays, Doubled Reverse Rays)** **I-3** **R-4**
Obverse II 1– Horizontal die gouge in rays below B in LIBERTY.
Reverse $\mathbf{B^1}$**a** – Slightly doubled rays on left side below tail feathers and below and above ONE.

1B **II 1 •** $\mathbf{B^1}$**a (Bar G)** **I-2** **R-5**
Obverse II 1– Vertical bar of shallow raised metal from left side of G of GOD down to near rim.

1C (Eliminated, became VAM 40)

•1D **II 1 •** $\mathbf{B^1}$**a (Vertical Die Gouge Between IN & GOD)** **I-3** **R-4**
Obverse II 1– Vertical die gouge through dot between N and G of IN GOD.

•1E/2L **II 1 •** $\mathbf{B^1}$**a (Slanted Die Gouge Between IB)** **I-3** **R-4**
Obverse II 1– Slanted die gouge in rays between I and B of LIBERTY.

•1H **II 1 •** $\mathbf{B^1}$**a (Bar Between N-G)** **I-2** **R-5**
Obverse II 1– Broad vertical die gouge between in N and G of IN GOD. Wider than VAMs 1B and 1D.

▫1I **II 1 •** $\mathbf{B^1}$**a (Die Chip Lower Back Hair Strand)** **I-2** **R-6**
Obverse II 1– Small die chip near tip of lower back hair strand.

□1J **II 1 • B¹a (Die Gouge Lower Olive Branch)** I-2 R-5
Reverse B¹a– Horizontal die gouge thru lower olive branch.

¶1M **II 1 • B¹a (Die Scratch at 9)** I-2 R-5
Obverse II 1– Thin vertical die scratch left of 9 and extending up to E in WE.

¶1P1 **II 1 • B²a (Double Die Gouges Below G)** I-2 R-6
Obverse II 1– Shallow vertical die gouges well below G in GOD.

▸1Q **II 1 • B¹a (Die Gouge Between N-G)** I-2 R-6
Obverse II 1– Shallow broad vertical die gouge from dot between N of IN and G of GOD down to rim. Different than VAMs 1B, 1D & 1H.

✚1S **II 1 • B¹a (Die Scratch 1)** I-2 R-4
Obverse II 1– Tiny vertical striated die scratch at 1 top left.

✗1U **II 1 • B¹a (Die Gouge VS)** I-2 R-5
Obverse II 1– Vertical die gouge below VS in TRVST.

✗1X **II 1 • B¹a (Small Rim Cud O)** I-2 R-6
Obverse II 1– Die marker- Faint thin vertical die scratch at third ray from front.
Reverse B¹a– Tiny shallow rim cud into field at O in ONE.

∇2E1(revised) **II 1 • B²a (Gouge Between 19)** I-2 R-5
Obverse II 1– Some specimens show shallow vertical die gouge bar between 1 and 9 in date.

✓2F(revised) **II 1 • B²a (Die Gouge in Rays Below E)** I-3 R-4
Obverse II 1– Horizontal die gouge in rays below E in LIBERTY. Later die states show shallow vertical die gouge below R in TRVST.

2H **II 1 • B²a (Die Gouge in Rays)** I-3 R-4
Obverse II 1– Slanted die gouge in rays below B of LIBERTY.

2J **II 1 • B²a (Bar R)** I-2 R-4
Obverse II 1– Vertical bar of shallow raised metal from R of TRVST down to rim due to die gouge.

2K **II 1 • B²a (Die Gouge Between B & E)** I-2 R-5
Obverse II 1– Horizontal die gouge in rays between B and E of LIBERTY.

•2M **II 1 • B²a (Vertical Die Gouge Between GO)** I-3 R-4
Obverse II 1– Vertical die gouge from between G and O of GOD down to rim.

•2N **II 1 • B²a (Die Gouge in Hair)** I-3 R-6
Obverse II 1– Horizontal die gouge in hair behind eye.

•2O **II 1 • B²a (Die Gouge Below E in LIBERTY)** I-3 R-6
Obverse II 1– Horizontal die gouge just below E in LIBERTY between two rays.

¶2P1(revised) **II 1 • B²a (Chin Bar)** I-3 R-5
Obverse II 1– Striated vertical die gouge down from Liberty head chin to right side of D in GOD and striated vertical die gouge left side of 1. Similar to 1923 P VAM 1F Chin Bar.

✚2P2 **II 1 • B²a (Chin Bar, Die Gouge 1, Die Scratch U)** I-3 R-5
Reverse B²a– Thin diagonal die scratch to right of U base in UNITED.

•2Q **II 1 • B²a (Die Gouge Above T)** I-2 R-6
Obverse II 1– Vertical die gouge from right top of T in TRVST up to lower horizontal hair strand.

✚2R1 **II 1 • B²a (Die Gouges Below GOD & TRVST)** I-2 R-6
Obverse II 1– Wide vertical die gouge below G in GOD and R in TRVST down near rim.

✚2R2 **II 1 • B²a (Die Gouges Below GOD & TRVST, Long Spike Eagle's Shoulder #4))** I-2 R-6
Obverse II 1– Wide vertical die gouges below G in GOD and R in TRVST down near rim.
Reverse B²a– Die clash long vertical spike up from eagle's right shoulder from back of neck of obverse up to right side of first U in UNUM.

•2S **II 1 • B²a (Triple Gouges Above IN)** I-2 R-5
Obverse II 1– Three shallow vertical die gouges above IN.

□2W **II 1 • B²a (Vertical Die Gouges Left Side of G)** I-2 R-6
Obverse II 1– Vertical die gouges and fine scratch lines from left side of G in GOD down to middle of field.

○2Y **II 1 • B²a (Diagonal Die Gouge Y)** I-2 R-6
Obverse II 1– Diagonal die gouge thru bottom of Y in LIBERTY.

○2Z **II 1 • B²a (Vertical Die Gouge N)** I-2 R-6
Obverse II 1– Wide and shallow vertical die gouge down from middle of oblique crossbar of N of IN.

○2AC **II 1 • B²a (Spiked Neck)** I-2 R-5
Obverse II 1– Thin horizontal die gouge thru point of Liberty head neck above 9.

∇2AD **II 1 • B²a (Die Gouge Below OD– Tail on O)** I-2 R-5
Obverse II 1– Diagonal die gouge from lower right of O to below D in GOD.

∇2AE **II 1 • B²a (Die Gouge DOLL)** I-2 R-5
Reverse B²a– Horizontal die gouge from right side of D thru OL to left side of second L in DOLLAR.

∇2AI **II 1 • B²a (Die Gouges Between ER)** I-2 R-5
Obverse II 1– Shallow horizontal die gouges at right of middle bar of E and left of R in LIBERTY.

§2AK **II 1 • B²a (Die Gouge Last Right Tall Ray)** I-2 R-5
Obverse II 1– Small horizontal die gouge thru top of last right tall ray between ER in LIBERTY.

✚2AL(revised) **II 1 • B²a (Die Gouge Rays Below E & Jaw)** I-2 R-5
Obverse II 1– Diagonal die gouge between four rays below E in LIBERTY and long gouge on jaw.

§2AM **II 1 • B²a (Die Gouge Back of Cheek, Separated Reverse Ray)** I-2 R-5
Obverse II 1– Horizontal die gouge back of cheek to hair and tiny short gouge just above it.
Reverse B²a– Vertical die file lines at top left and right fields with second ray shortened from top above eagle and separated at wing edge.

§2AS(revised) **II 1 • B²a (Die Scratch Next to Last Ray)** I-2 R-6
Obverse II 1– Long thin and shallow horizontal die scratch at base of next to last right ray. Same die as VAM 2AG.
Reverse B²a– Die changed after severe clash of VAM 2AG.

§2AU1 **II 1 • B²a (Die Gouge T)** I-2 R-5
Obverse II 1– Very short horizontal die gouge from neck to T in TRVST.

§2AW **II 1 • B²a (Die Scratch in Headband)** I-2 R-5
Obverse II 1– Thin diagonal die scratch at rear of headband.

§2AX **II 1 • B²a (Die Gouge G Right Side)** I-2 R-6
Obverse II 1– Long shallow and wide vertical die gouge thru right side of G in GOD.

#2BJ **II 1 • B²a (Diagonal Die Gouge Front Rays)** I-2 R-5
Obverse II 1– Broad and shallow diagonal die gouge between second and third tall rays from front.

#2BL **II 1 • B²a (Die Scratches Thru S)** I-2 R-5
Obverse II 1– Double vertical die gouges thru, above and below S in TRVST.

#2BM **II 1 • B²a (Die Gouge Olive Leaf)** I-2 R-5
Reverse B²a– Broad diagonal die gouge on right olive leaf cluster that removes stems of top leaf and berry. Some heavy die scratches thru top olive leaf.

#2BO **II 1 • B²a (Die Gouge Rear Hair Strands)** I-2 R-5
Obverse II 1– Horizontal die gouge between top two rear hair strands.

#2BP **II 1 • B²a (Close Double Clash Spikes Eagle's Shoulder, Die Gouges UNITED)** I-3 R-5
Reverse B²a– Clashed die with close double long vertical spikes from right side of eagle's shoulder. Spikes further right than VAM 2AQ. Shallow diagonal die gouges in UNITED.

#2BQ **II 1 • B²a (Horizontal Die Scratch Below WE)** I-2 R-4
Obverse II 1– Thin horizontal die scratch in field below WE.

¶2BV **II 1 • B²a (Diagonal Die Gouge Inside O of GOD)** I-2 R-5
Obverse II 1– Shallow diagonal die gouge at right inside of O in GOD.

¶2BW **II 1 • B²a (Die Scratch Above DOL)** I-2 R-5
Reverse B²a– Long fine horizontal die scratch above DOL in DOLLAR.

▸2BZ **II 1 • B²a (Beveled Field)** I-2 R-6
Obverse II 1– Beveled field next to rim below RVS.
Reverse B²a– Very slightly doubled top of eagle's right shoulder.

▸2CB **II 1 • B²a (Die Gouge WE)** I-2 R-5
Obverse II 1– Small horizontal die gouge thru middle of WE.
Reverse B²a– Some fine die rust pits and scratches in left field.

✓2CC(revised) **II 1 • B²a (Die File Lines Neck, Die Gouges Below RV)** I- 2 R-5
Obverse II 1– Diagonal die file lines across middle of Liberty head neck and thru TRVST. Three shallow vertical die gouges below RV.
Reverse B²a– Die file lines above eagle's left wing and at eagle's right shoulder to remove die clash marks.

✓2CG **II 1 • B²e (Die Scratch Eye)** I-2 R-5
Obverse II 1– Vertical die scratch at back of eye.

✓2CH **II 1 • B²a (Die Gouge Right of 2)** I-2 R-5
Obverse II 1– Short die gouge at rim to right of right 2.

✓2CN **II 1 • B²a (Extra Ray Below Upper Tail Feathers)** I-2 R-4
Reverse B²a– Short die gouge just above top ray below eagle's tail feathers with appearance of an extra ray.

✚2CQ **II 1 • B²a (Die Gouge G Middle)** I-2 R-5
Obverse II 1– Faint short, vertical narrow die gouges below middle of G in GOD.

✚2CR1 **II 1 • B²a (Die Gouge G Left)** I-2 R-5
Obverse II 1– Striated vertical narrow die gouge below left side of G in GOD. Not as far left as VAM 2W.

✚2CU **II 1 • B²a (Die Scratches OD)** I-2 R-5
Obverse II 1– Two long vertical die scratches down from OD in GOD.

✚2CW **II 1 • B²a (Die Gouges Below OD)** I-2 R-5
Obverse II 1– Broad vertical die gouges below OD in GOD.

✚2CX **II 1 • B²a (Long Spike Eagle's Shoulder)** I-2 R-5
Obverse II 1– Narrow slightly beveled field at 1.
Reverse B²a– Long vertical raised clash spike up from eagle's right shoulder close to neck from back of neck of obverse up to barely reaching eagle's beak at bottom of U.

✗2DD **II 1 • B²a (Collar Clash Reverse)** I-2 R-5
Obverse II 1– *Die marker*- Faint vertical die gouge below IN.
Reverse B²a– Collar clash of reeding on rim below mountains.

✗2DE **II 1 • B²a (Die Gouges GOD)** I-2 R-5
Obverse II 1– Numerous die gouges and scratches above and below GOD.

✗2DG **II 1 • B²a (Die Gouges Cheek)** I-3 R-6
Obverse II 1– Horizontal segmented 7 short die gouges in line across face back of nose to hair.

✗2DH **II 1 • B²a (Die Scratches Arc DO)** I-3 R-6
Reverse B²a– Vertical arc of parallel short die scratches from left side of D in DOLLAR up to edge of eagle's wing above O. A few parallel short die scratches above olive sprig.

✗2DM **II 1 • B²a (Die Gouge IN)** I-2 R-5
Obverse II 1– Vertical die gouge between I & N of IN.

✗2DQ **II 1 • B²a (Die Gouge Below GO, Long Clash Spike)** I-2 R-6
Obverse II 1– Vertical die gouge well below GO in GOD with smooth shiny patch on left side.
Reverse B²a– Die clash with long raised spike up from eagle's right shoulder from back of neck of obverse up to bottom of N in UNUM with weak top. Similar to VAM 2BY/2AB.

✗3(revised) **II 1 • B²b (Doubled Leg Feathers, Die Gouge Forehead)** I-3 R-4
Obverse II 1– Small die gouge at top edge of Liberty forehead.

Reverse B^2b– Lower leg feathers doubled on left side with rear one tripled. Doubled left olive leaves and couple of feathers on left edge of eagle's middle left side.

◊5-2 **II 1 • B^2c (Tripled Olive Leaves, Die Gouge G)** **I-3** **R-5**

Obverse II 1– Vertical die gouge above and below G in GOD.

◊5A1 **II 1 • B^2c (Tripled Olive Leaves, Die Gouge G)** **I-3** **R-6**

Obverse II 1– Vertical die gouge above and below G in GOD. Different obverse die than VAMs 5, 5B & 5C.

Reverse B^2c– *Die marker*– Die wear lines thru E in ONE. Same die as VAMs 5 & 5C but earliest die state.

◊5C **II 1 • B^2c (Rusted Face, Tripled Olive Leaves)** **I-2** **R-6**

Obverse II 1– Raised dots and splotches from rusted die on cheek, neck and above date. Faint vertical die gouge above and below G in GOD. Different die than VAMs 5, 5A & 5B.

Reverse B^2c– *Die marker*– Die wear lines thru E in ONE. Same die as VAMs 5 & 5A. Latest die state.

✓18(revised) **II 1 • B^2n (Doubled Talons at Bottom)** **I-3** **R-5**

Obverse II 1– Beveled field next to rim below IN GOD RVS from damaged die. Slightly doubled top inside of 2's upper loop and designer's initials.

Reverse B^2n– Eagle's two talons of right leg doubled at bottom. Lower olive branch doubled on left side. Slightly doubled top left olive leaf and top olive on left side, lower olive leaf of middle sprig at bottom, lower left olive leaf on right side, leg feathers on back side, top of eagle's right shoulder, first and third ray above E of ONE on left side, rays above DOLLA and rays below DOLL on right side.

✚22A **II 8 • B^2a (Doubled 922 & Motto, Beveled Field RVST)** **I-3** **R-6**

Obverse II 8– Beveled field with gouges next to rim below RVST.

◊25B **II 1 • B^2s (Doubled Right Talon & Olive Leaves, Die Gouges Below IN-G)** **I-3** **R-6**

Obverse II 1– Six vertical die gouges below IN-G with slightly beveled field at rim below gouges.

▸29A **II 10 • B^2w (Doubled 922, Doubled Reverse Rays, Gouges Below IN)** **I-3** **R-6**

Obverse II 10– Shallow vertical die gouges below IN at right side of N and below left side of N.

♯31A **II 11 • B^2a (Doubled Rt. Tiara Rays & Liberty Head Profile, Die Gouges Above IN)** **I-2** **R-5**

Obverse II 11– Narrow shallow vertical die gouges above IN.

✚34A **II 1 • B^2aa (Doubled Lower Right Reverse, Die Gouges Right 2)** **I-3** **R-4**

Obverse II 1– Several vertical die gouges on left side of right 2.

∇39 **II 1 • B^1c (Doubled ONE, Die Gouge Rays)** **I-3** **R-5**

Obverse II 1– Same horizontal die gouge in rays below B of LIBERTY as VAM 1A, but later die state.

Reverse B^1c– Slightly doubled ONE, three rays above and three rays below on left side. Very slightly doubled rays below tail feathers on left side.

∇40 **II 1 • B^1d (Doubled Lower Reverse, Die Gouge in Rays)** **I-3** **R-4**

Obverse II 1– Horizontal die gouge in rays low between BE of LIBERTY on some specimens. (Formerly VAM 1C)

Reverse B^1d– Slightly doubled lower olive leaves on left side, back of rear-most leg feather, rays below tail feathers on left side, three rays above and three rays below ONE and left side of ON in ONE.

▸54A **II 1 • B^2am (Doubled Olive Leaves & Rays, Die Gouge N)** **I-2** **R-6**

Obverse II 1– Shallow vertical die gouge below right side of N of IN.

1922 D

▫1F1 **II 1 • B^1a (Spiked Eye)** **I-3** **R-6**

Obverse II 1– Thin, long, slightly slanted die gouge thru eye.

∇1P **II 1 • B^1a (Shallow Die Gouge Between IB)** **I-2** **R-5**

Obverse II 1– Shallow short die gouge thru 5th tall ray from front between IE of LIBERTY.

✚1AA **II 1 • B^1a (Die Gouge W, Die Scratch Chin)** **I-2** **R-5**

Obverse II 1– Short vertical die gouge from jaw down to left top of W in WE. Long thin vertical die scratch from nostril down to front of chin.

○2W **II 1 • B^2a (Bar N Die Gouge)** **I-2** **R-5**

Obverse II 1– Shallow wide vertical die gouge below N of IN down to rim.

✗2BJ **II 1 • B^2a (Die Gouge L, Die Break Below Hair Strands)** **I-3** **R-6**

Obverse II 1– Long diagonal die gouge below L in LIBERTY. Die crack from neck thru left T in TRVST up to lower rear hair strand with displaced field break below hair strands.

✗2BO **II 1 • B^2a (Die Gouge Below G)** **I-2** **R-5**

Obverse II 1– Diagonal die gouge at rim below G in GOD.

✚5(revised) **II 3 • B^1a (Bar 2, Doubled Designer's Initials)** **I-3** **R-5**

Obverse II 3– Slight doubling of de Francisci's monogram, upper inside of both 2 loops and lower edge of TR in TRVST. Vertical die gouge from top of right 2 up to neck.

7 **II 1 • B^2d (Tripled Reverse)** **I-3** **R-5**

Obverse II 1– Small diagonal die gouge in front tiara and short one at back of hair.

Reverse B^2d– Tripled lower edge of olive leaves, eagle's right talon plus back of rear leg feathers. Doubled lower edge of olive branch, DO in DOLLAR, and eagle's middle talon.

▸8(revised) **II 1 • B^2e (Doubled Wing, Die Gouge B)** **I-3** **R-5**

Obverse II 1– Semi-circular die gouge at rim to left of B in LIBERTY.

Reverse B^2e– Doubled edge of eagle's right wing, lower edges of DO in DOLLAR, lower edge of upper olive branches and middle of eagle's right talons.

¶13B **II 1 • B^2h (Tripled Lower Right Reverse, Die Scratch Talon)** **I-2** **R-6**

Reverse B^2h– Diagonal die scratch thru eagle's middle talon.

1922 S

•1A **II 1 • B^1a (Shortened Tiara Ray, Die Gouge I)** **I-3** **R-4**

Obverse II 1– Bottom of first six rays in Tiara are over polished and missing as are leading hair strands adjacent to them. Some pitting around loop of left 2 due to rusted die. Wide diagonal die gouge thru I of LIBERTY with many fine lines.

✗1AD **II 1 • B^{1}a (Die Gouge A)** **I-2 R-5**
Reverse B^{1}a– Diagonal die gouge thru top of A in DOLLAR.

2A **II 1 • B^{2}a** (Spiked Tail Feather) **I-3 R-6**
Reverse B^{2}a– Diagonal die gouge at the end of the tail feathers.

✚2C1(revised) **II 1 • B^{2}a (Flaming Ray Die Gouge Above ONE, Double Clash Spikes Eagle's Shoulder)** **I-3 R-6**
Reverse B^{2}a– Diagonal wide die gouge from top of first ray above ONE. Polished double clash spikes up from eagle's right shoulder.

▫2D/2J1 **II 1 • B^{2}a (Worm Die Gouge Thru G)** **I-2 R-5**
Obverse II 1– Irregular worm-like die gouge that goes vertically thru G in GOD and above it but slants diagonally to right below G. (Same as VAM 2J1?)

∇2E **II 1 • B^{2}a (Die Gouge Front Rays)** **I-2 R-5**
Obverse II 1– Vertical die gouge between 1 & 2 long rays in front of Tiara.

§2 I **II 1 • B^{2}a (Die Scratch W)** **I-2 R-5**
Obverse II 1– Fine line diagonal die scratch thru right side of W in WE.

◊2J1 **III^{2}1 • B^{2}a (Die Gouges G, R & T)** **I-3 R-5**
Obverse II 1– Curved vertical die gouge thru G in Gòd, gouge at bottom right of R in LIBERTY and faint vertical gouge at top of left T in TRVST.

#2K(revised) **II 1 • B^{2}a (Triple Clash Spikes Eagle's Shoulder #2, Scratches in B)** **I-2 R-5**
Obverse II 1– Long vertical die scratches thru B in LIBERTY.
Reverse B^{2}a– Triple clash spikes up from eagle's right shoulder with middle spike weak and close to right one.

§2M **II 1 • B^{2}a (Die Gouge Left Wing Tip)** **I-2 R-5**
Reverse B^{2}a– Horizontal die gouge at base of third ray from top of eagle's left wing.

§2N/2AG **II 1 • B^{2}a (Missing Reverse Rays Middle)** **I-3 R-5**
Reverse B^{2}a– Clashed die with heavy die file lines in right and left fields with portions of rays missing to right of O and L in DOLLAR and above L.

✓2U **II 1 • B^{2}a (Die Gouge Below WE)** **I-2 R-5**
Obverse II 1– Slightly curved diagonal die gouge from Liberty head neck over under WE.

✚2Z **II 1 • B^{2}a (Die Scratch Hair Bun)** **I-2 R-5**
Obverse II 1– Vertical thin die scratch from top of Liberty head hair bun up towards rim.

◊2AB **II 1 • B^{2}a (Die Gouge Below AR)** **I-2 R-6**
Reverse B^{1}a– Diagonal die gouge at rim below AR in DOLLAR.

✗2AI **II 1 • B^{2}a (Die Gouges Front Rays)** **I-2 R-5**
Obverse II 1– Several shallow vertical die gouges at tops of first five front long rays.

✚5A(revised) **II 1 • B^{2}c (Doubled Eagle's Neck & Wing, Missing Reverse Rays)** **I-4 R-6**
Obverse II 1– Diagonal die scratch above left 2.
Reverse B^{2}c– Fine polishing lines to remove die clash marks which resulted in missing or weakened portions of rays below DOL.

1923 P

✓1C(revised) **II 1 • B^{2}a (Tail on O, Die Break Rear of Tiara Rays, Collar Clash)** **I-4 R-6**
Obverse II 1– Short thin diagonal die break to right of last ray in Tiara. Shallow wide vertical die gouge thru bottom of S to rim in TRVST.
Reverse B^{2}a– Die break from lower part of O in DOLLAR extending diagonally down to left. Collar clash on rim below and to right of LAR.

1F1 **II 1 • B^{2}a (Chin Bar)** **I-3 R-5**
Obverse II 1– Vertical bar of shallow raised metal from chin down right side of D motto to top of 1 due to die gouge.

○1G(revised) **II 1 • B^{2}a (Die Gouge in Rays & Below O)** **I-3 R-4**
Obverse II 1– Horizontal die gouge in rays below B of LIBERTY. Later die states show a shallow broad vertical die gouge below O in GOD down to rim.

1 I **II 1 • B^{2}a (Die Gouge in LIBERTY)** **I-3 R-4**
Obverse II 1– Slanted die gouge through top part of E of LIBERTY.

1J **II 1 • B^{2}a (Die Gouge in Rays)** **I-3 R-4**
Obverse II 1– Diagonal die gouge through third long ray to right of I in LIBERTY with raised dot below right end of die gouge.

1K **II 1 • B^{2}a (Die Gouge in E of LIBERTY)** **I-3 R-5**
Obverse II 1– Slanted die gouge through top part of E of LIBERTY similar to VAM 1 I but shorter line on left side of E and longer line on right side of E.

1L1 **II 1 • B^{2}a (Die Gouge in 5th Left Ray)** **I-3 R-5**
Obverse II 1– Diagonal die gouge through fifth long ray from left of Liberty's tiara.

1M **II 1 • B^{2}a (Die Gouge in Rays Well Below E)** **I-3 R-5**
Obverse II 1– Horizontal die gouge in rays well below E in LIBERTY next to hair.

•1N **II 1 • B^{2}a (Die Gouges Below GOD)** **I-2 R-6**
Obverse II 1– Vertical striated die gouges below G and D in GOD. Small diagonal die gouge in hair below E in LIBERTY.

•1P **II 1 • B^{2}a (Die Gouge R in LIBERTY)** **I-3 R-5**
Obverse II 1– Diagonal die gouge at lower left of R in LIBERTY.

∗1Q **II 1 • B^{2}a (Die Gouge in Rays Below Tail)** **I-2 R-5**
Reverse B^{2}a– Small horizontal die gouge in rays extending from rear talon to eagle's tail feathers.

∗1R **II 1 • B^{2}a (Die Gouge in Upper Hair)** **I-2 R-5**
Obverse II 1– Small horizontal die gouge in upper hair just above and to right of eye.

▫1T1 **II 1 • B^{2}a (Die Gouge in Lower Olive Leaves)** **I-2 R-6**
Reverse B^{2}a– Thin horizontal die gouge on either side of lower left olive leaf.

▫1U **II 1 • B^{2}a (Die Gouge Below O)** **I-2 R-5**
Obverse II 1– Vertical striated die gouge below O in GOD down to rim.

○1X **II 1 • B^{2}a (Bar S Die Gouge)** **I-2 R-5**
Obverse II 1– Shallow wide vertical die gouge thru bottom of S down to rim in TRVST.

#1Z(revised) **II 1 • B^2a (Damaged Die Below TRVST)** I-4 R-5

Obverse II 1– Raised field patch below RV in TRVST and pushed-in rim from damaged die. Some heavy die file lines around TRVST in attempt to remove damage.

✚1AB1 II 1 • B^2a (Beveled Field Below TRVST) I-3 R-4

Obverse II 1– Beveled field next to rim below TRVST from damaged die. (Formerly VAM 1AU.)

¶1AC1 II 1 • B^2a (X Die Scratches Below Talons) I-2 R-6

Reverse B^2a– Two die scratches in form of an X shape below eagle's right foot between the talons.

✓1AD(revised) **II 1 • B^2a (Rim Cuds at Date, Die Gouges Above T)** I-3 R-6

Obverse II 1– Four die breaks on rim below date that extend into field with one almost touching bottom of 9. Two short vertical gouges above and to right of right T in TRVST.

§1AG II 1 • B^2a (Diagonal Die Scratch O) I-2 R-5

Obverse II 1– Diagonal die scratch thru O in GOD up to above G.

§1AI1 II 1 • B^2a (Die Gouge Above Second T in TRVST) I-2 R-5

Obverse II 1– Short broad vertical die gouge at top of second T in TRVST.

§1AJ II 1 • B^2a (Die Gouge Thru Reverse Ray) I-2 R-5

Reverse B^2a– Short shallow die gouge across lower part of third ray from top above eagle.

§1AK II 1 • B^2a (Die Scratches NE) I-2 R-5

Reverse B^2a– Faint diagonal die scratches below NE.

§1AM II 1 • B^2a (Die Scratches 1) I- 2 R-5

Obverse II 1– Diagonal die scratches at left top of 1.

§1AO II 1 • B^2a (Die Gouge Right of E in LIBERTY) I-2 R-5

Obverse II 1– Slanted short shallow die gouge to right of base of E in LIBERTY.

#1AS II 1 • B^2a (Die Gouge Thru RV) I-2 R-5

Obverse II 1– Broad shallow vertical die gouge thru RV in TRVST extending up to hair and below RV.

¶1BA II 1 • B^2a (Gouge 9) I-2 R-5

Obverse II 1– Vertical die gouge on left side of 9 upper loop.

¶1BC II 1 • B^2a (Gouge Above Eagle's Neck) I-2 R-5

Reverse B^2a– Broad and shallow diagonal die gouge above eagle's neck.

▸1BE II 1 • B^2a (Impaled Eye) I-3 R-5

Obverse II 1– Short wide horizontal die gouge at front of eye. Faint diagonal die scratch thru nose.

▸1BF II 1 • B^2a (Die Gouge Thru Right T in TRVST) I-2 R-5

Obverse II 1– Shallow wide vertical striated die gouge thru right side of right T in TRVST.

▸1BG II 1 • B^2a (Beveled Field Below 23) I-2 R-5

Obverse II 1– Beveled field next to rim below 23 from damaged die.

▸1BH1 II 1 • B^2a (Die Scratch Below E) I-2 R-5

Obverse II 1– Diagonal die scratch in hair below E in LIBERTY.

▸1BI II 1 • B^2a (Die Scratch Between TE) I-2 R-4

Reverse B^2a– Vertical die scratch between TE of UNITED that extends into E middle bar.

✓1BL II 1 • B^2a (Die Gouge Below Eagle's Beak) I-2 R-5

Reverse B^2a– Possible short shallow horizontal die gouge from neck below eagle's beak..

✓1BM II 1 • B^2a (Die Gouges Below OD) I-2 R-6

Obverse II 1– Vertical striated die gouges below OD in GOD. Similar to VAM 1N but further to right.

✚1BO II 1 • B^2a (Die Gouges Above Right T) I-2 R-5

Obverse II 1– Three vertical die gouges at rim above right T in TRVST with middle one faint.

✚1BR II 1 • B^2a (Striated Gouge Above N) I-2 R-5

Obverse II 1– Striated vertical die gouge above N of IN.

◇1BS II 1 • B^2a (Die Scratch 9) I-2 R-5

Obverse II 1– Long diagonal die scratch from 9 top up to below W in WE and continuing shortly above W.

◇1BT II 1 • B^2a (Die Gouge RV) I-2 R-6

Obverse II 1– Thin vertical die gouge to rim below RV in TRVST.

✗1BY II 1 • B^2a (Polished Triangle 19) I-2 R-6

Obverse II 1– Polished triangle between 1 & 9 from feed finger contact.

✗1CB II 1 • B^2a (Die Gouges Above IN) I-2 R-5

Obverse II 1– Two vertical die gouges above IN from feed finger.

♮1CC II 1 • B^2a (Die Gouges Left Obverse Rim) I-2 R-5

Obverse II 1– Vertical die gouges from rim at K-8 & K-9.

♮1CF II 1 • B^2a (Beveled 3) I-2 R-5

Obverse II 1– Small beveled field below 3 from feed fingers contact.

♮1CH II 1 • B^2a (Die Gouges N & G) I-2 R-5

Obverse II 1– Short vertical die gouges below N & G of IN GOD from feed fingers.

▸4A II 1 • B^2a (Doubled Middle Reverse, Beveled Field Below RVST) I-3 R-6

Obverse II 1– Beveled field next to rim below RVST and small beveled bar to right of T next to rim. Narrower beveling than VAMs 1Z & 1AU.

◇7A II^1 • B^2f (Doubled Reverse Rays, Gouge Above Right T) I-3 R-6

Obverse II 1– Vertical die gouge at rim above right T in TRVST.

○11 II 1 • B^2i (Doubled Middle Olive Leaves) I-2 R-5

Obverse II 1– Short horizontal die gouge tick at upper front of neck above E.

Reverse B^2i– Slightly doubled middle olive leaves on lower side, back of two rear leg feathers and left side of three rays above ONE.

1923 D

¶1A(revised) **II 1 • B²a (Die Gouge Thru S in STATES, Die Break Top of Y)** **I-3 R-6**

Obverse II 1– Die crack from hair bun thru middle of Y vertical bar of LIBERTY and up thru right top of Y to rim where it splits into two lines with displaced field die break on later die state.

Reverse B²a– Diagonal die gouge thru left S in STATES.

#1D1 **II 1 • B²a (Die Gouge Below Neck)** **I-2 R-5**

Obverse II 1– Vertical shallow die gouge from designer's initials down to between 2 & 3.

§1G(revised) **II 1 • B²a (Die Break Back of Hair, Die Gouge Reverse Rays)** **I-2 R-6**

Obverse II 1– Late die states have long circular die crack from hair bun down to RV in TRVST with displaced field above horizontal hair strands.

Reverse B²a– Long thin horizontal die gouge from eagle's right wing thru rays above OLLA.

○1V **II 1 • B²a (Die Gouge Below B)** **I-2 R-5**

Obverse II 1– Diagonal die gouge in rays below B in LIBERTY.

#1AG(revised) **II 1 • B²a (Die Break Right of Y #3)** **I-2 R-6**

Obverse B²a– Die break from rim at top right of Y in LIBERTY with die crack thru Y just below middle junction. Late die states also have vertical polished area with lines in front of nose and lips and below chin.

§1AN **II 1 • B²a (Die Scratch Fifth Tall Ray From Front)** **I-2 R-5**

Obverse II 1– Horizontal thin and shallow die scratch thru fifth tall ray from front.

✚1AO1 **II 1 • B²a (Die Gouges Back of Tiara Band & Eye)** **I-3 R-6**

Obverse II 1– Multiple lines in wide die gouge at rear of tiara band and several diagonal die gouges at eye front. (Formerly VAM 1BU.)

✚1AX1 **• B²a (Die Gouge Below E)** **I-2 R-5**

Obverse II 1-- Vertical die gouge below E in WE.

✓1BI **II 1 • B²a (Die Gouge 3)** **I-2 R-5**

Obverse II 1– Short vertical die gouge at left side of 3. Some die file lines in top fields.

✚1BK1 **II 1 • B²a (Chin Bar)** **I-2 R-5**

Obverse II 1– Vertical die gouge down from Liberty head chin down to top right of D in GOD. Some light striated vertical bars in front of lips and chin.

◇1BK2 **II 1 • B²a (Chin Bar, Die Gouge TY)** **I-2 R-6**

Obverse II 1– Diagonal die gouge between middle right of T and upper left of Y in LIBERTY. Very late die state with weakened chin bar die gouge.

◇1BK3 **II 1 • B²a (Chin Bar, Die Gouges Obverse)** **I-5 R-7**

Obverse II 1– Numerous die gouges/scratches including diagonal die gouge between middle right of T and upper left of Y in LIBERTY, at RVST and above thru rear hair strands, around LI in LIBERTY, nose, lips, face, upper neck and top of 3. Most extensive die gouges/scratches on a Peace dollar.

✚1BS **II 1 • B²a (Hooked Liberty Lip)** **I-5 R-7**

Obverse II 1– Multiple long horizontal die gouges and scratches on left field and face. Long horizontal die gouge from rim over to Liberty head upper lip and double lines bent upwards behind lip with striations in front of lip. Long horizontal die scratch with double lines from rim above gouge over to nose, across cheek and down to rear jaw-neck junction. Third single line die scratch from rim below L over thru eye to hair edge. Fourth die scratch from jaw-neck junction into hair and making sharp turn upwards and diagonally forward in hair. Heavy die file lines at rim from IN to 1. Die likely retired very early.

◇1CB **II 1 • B²a (K-3 Rim Cud #8)** **I-2 R-6**

Obverse II 1– Die crack thru upper part of top left leg of Y in LIBERTY with sharp turn up to rim on left side and continuing to right thru middle of vee over to right and up shortly to rim with displaced field cud break. Some horizontal die scratches at back of rear ray.

◇1CC **II 1 • B²a (Die Gouges 3 & E)** **I-2 R-5**

Obverse II 1– Shallow vertical die gouge on left side of 3 and long thin shallow die gouge below E in WE.

◇1CE **II 1 • B²a (Scraped Obverse)** **I-2 R-5**

Obverse II 1– Shiny vertical bars at left edge of Liberty head neck and between 9 & 2 of scraped die.

✗1CF **II 1 • B²a (Gouges Lips & Jaw)** **I-3 R-6**

Obverse II 1– Couple vertical die gouge at lips and several short vertical die gouges at jaw edge from feed fingers.

1923 S

▫1H **II 1 • B²a (Die Gouge 2)** **I-2 R-5**

Obverse II 1– Diagonal die gouge thru middle of 2.

§1V **II 1 • B²a (Die Gouge US)** **I-2 R-5**

Reverse B²a– Vertical die gouge from top of eagle's head up to between US in PLURIBUS.

◇1AD3 **II 1 • B²a (Triple Clash Spikes Eagle's Shoulder #3, Die Scratches Y & 2)** **I-2 R-5**

Obverse II 1– Striated horizontal die scratch added above 2.

#1AO **II 1 • B²a (Short Gouge Third Tall Front Ray)** **I-2 R-5**

Obverse II 1– Thin short die gouge on left side of third tall ray from front of tiara.

¶1AQ1 **II 1 • B²a (Shallow Die Gouge B)** **I-2 R-5**

Obverse II 1– Shallow long die gouge above short ray to right of B in LIBERTY.

✚1AZ(revised) **II 1 • B²a (Shortened Front Two Rays)** **I-2 R-5**

Obverse II 1– Front of hair over polished with slightly beveled field and first two rays shortened away from hair. *Die marker*– Two horizontal polishing lines at rear tiara ray.

Reverse B²a– Vertical and horizontal die file lines at clash mark at olive leaves.

✚1BI **II 1 • B²a (Die Scratch N, Die File Lines Reverse)** **I-2 R-5**

Reverse B²a– Horizontal die scratch from lower right of N in UNITED. Die file lines at die clash marks.

✚1BK **II 1 • B²a (Die Scratch E)** **I-2 R-5**

Obverse II 1– Short diagonal die scratch at left side of E in LIBERTY thru adjacent ray.

◊1BW **II 1 • B²a (Die Scratches Last Three Obverse Rays)** I-2 R-5
Obverse II 1– Several short horizontal die scratches at three last rays.

◊1BX **II 1 • B²a (Die Gouges Front Ray & Left of B)** I-2 R-5
Obverse II 1– Short vertical die gouge at base of front ray and at rim between 5th & 6th long rays from front. Slightly polished and beveled field at front ray.

♮1CP **II 1 • B²a (Die Gouge Ray B)** I-2 R-5
Obverse II 1– Vertical die gouge on long ray left of B in LIBERTY.

♮1CR **II 1 • B²a (Die Gouges ER, Die Break L-IN)** I-2 R-5
Obverse II 1– Vertical shallow die gouges up from top of hair to rim between ER in LIBERTY. Die crack from L down to IN with die file lines and displaced field break.

1924 P

1A1 **II 1 • B²a (Bar D)** I-3 R-5
Obverse II 1– Vertical bar of shallow metal from left side of D in motto down to left side of 1 due to die gouge.

•1E **II 1 • B²a (Die Scratch Thru G in GOD)** I-2 R-6
Obverse II 1– Long thin vertical die scratch thru G in GOD extending upwards in front of lip and down to near rim.

✶1F **II 1 • B²a (Bar V)** I-2 R-6
Obverse II 1– Wide and shallow vertical double die gouges below V in TRVST down to rim.

▫1J **II 1 • B²a (Die Gouge in Lower Olive Leaves)** I-2 R-6
Reverse B²a– Thick diagonal die gouge thru lower left olive leaves.

▫1K1 **II 1 • B²a (Die Gouge Thru Left Side of G in GOD)** I-2 R-6
Obverse II 1– Long, medium width, vertical die gouge thru left side of G in GOD. Set further left than VAM 1E. Faint second vertical die gouge just to left one above G.

▫1L **II 1• B²a (Vertical Die Gouge Left of G)** I-2 R-6
Obverse II 1– Striated vertical die gouge on left outside of G in GOD that extends down to rim and up above G.

○1M **II 1 • B²a (Vertical Die Gouge Below O & Left of G)** I-2 R-5
Obverse II 1– Striated vertical die gouge below O in GOD and faint vertical die gouge left of G similar to VAM 1L.

∇1N **II 1 • B²a (Vertical Die Gouge S)** I-2 R-6
Obverse II 1– Wide and shallow vertical die gouge bar thru S in TRVST.

∇1 O **II 1 • B²a (Vertical Gouge Between 1 & 9)** I-2 R-5
Obverse II 1– Shallow and narrow die gouge between 1 and 9.

§1S **II 1 • B²a (Die Gouge Between O & D)** I-2 R-5
Obverse II 1– Short shallow die gouge between O and D in GOD that extends slightly above and below D. Not as long and low as VAM 1A.

§1U **II 1 • B²a (Die Gouge Below N)** I-2 R-5
Obverse II 1– Short vertical die wear gouge below right side of N of IN.

§1Y **II 1 • B²a (Vertical Die Gouge Between VS)** I-2 R-5
Obverse II 1– Wide and shallow vertical die gouge between V & S in TRVST.

§1Z **II 1 • B²a (Vertical Die Gouge Right of G)** I-2 R-5
Obverse II 1– Long vertical die gouge at right edge of G in GOD. Further right than VAMs 1E, 1L & 1M.

♯1AD **II 1 • B²a (Cut Throat Die Scratch)** I-2 R-5
Obverse II 1– Horizontal thin die scratch a front of jaw-neck junction.

¶1AI **II 1 • B²a (Vertical Die Gouges Below VS)** I-2 R-5
Obverse II 1– Narrow and short vertical shallow die gouges below V, between VS and below S in TRVST.

¶1AJ **II 1 • B²a (Gouges Below & Above S)** I-2 R-5
Obverse II 1– Narrow short vertical die gouges at left of bottom of S in TRVST, one thru lower left of S, one above S and one to right of S.

¶1AL **II 1 • B²a (Triple Die Gouges Below G)** I-2 R-5
Obverse II 1– Wide triple vertical die gouges well below G right side.

✚1AP **II 1 • B²a (Die Scratches W)** I-2 R-5
Obverse II 1– Vertical die scratches at top left of W in WE.

✚1AR **II 1 • B²a (Die Gouges 24 & Eagle's Wing, Pitted Reverse)** I-3 R-5
Obverse II 1– Small short vertical die gouge at rim between 24.
Reverse B²a– Two wide diagonal die gouges at eagle's left wing edge. Raised dots from rusted die in field above gouges.

✚1AS **II 1 • B²a (Pitted Obverse # 6)** I-2 R-6
Obverse II 1– Raised dots and splotches in field in front of Liberty head. *Die marker*– Fine horizontal die scratch thru top of 9.

✚1AT **II 1 • B²a (Spiked Forehead)** I-3 R-6
Obverse II 1– Long horizontal die scratch in field in front of Liberty head forehead.

✚1AU **II 1 • B²a (Die Gouge O)** I-2 R-5
Obverse II 1– Vertical shallow and broad die gouge thru O in GOD.

✚1AV **II 1 • B²a (Die Gouge Thru N)** I-2 R-5
Obverse II 1 – Short vertical die gouge thru middle of N of IN.

✚1AY **II 1 • B²a (Die Scratch Behind Rays)** I-2 R-5
Obverse II 1– Diagonal die scratch in hair behind tiara rays.

◊1BE **II 1 • B²a (Die Scratches Face)** I-2 R-5
Obverse II 1– Horizontal die scratch at back of Liberty head face near hair and couple short diagonal die scratches above nearby edge of hair.

♮1BT **II 1 • B²a (Die Gouge RV)** I-2 R-5
Obverse II 1– Vertical broad die gouge below RV in TRVST.

✚8B(revised) **II 1 • B²a (Shortened Reverse Rays, Gouged Eye)** I-3 R-5
Obverse II 1– Different obverse die from VAMs 8 & 8A without die file lines above TRV or die clash bars below R in LIBERTY. Short diagonal die gouge at lower front of eye. Some faint raised dots of rusted die at to loop of 9.
Reverse B²a– Later die state than VAMs 8 & 8A.

1924 S

#1C2 **II 1 • B^2a (Die Scratch T, Collar Clash)** I-2 R-5
Reverse B^2a– Thin die scratch at top left of T in LIBERTY.(Formerly VAM 1F.)

✚1I **II 1 • B^2a (Beveled Field Date, Die File Lines Obverse)** I-2 R-5
Obverse II 1– Die file lines at top field and at date with beveled field below date.

◊1J **II 1 • B^2a (Die Gouge Below Eagle's Foot)** I-2 R-5
Reverse B^2a– Horizontal die gouge below eagle's right foot.

♮1L **II 1 • B^2a (Die Gouges Hair Edge)** I-2 R-5
Obverse II 1– Short horizontal die gouges at hair edge behind eye and two at back of jaw.

✚3(revised) **II 1 • B^2c (Doubled Lower Reverse)** I-3 R-4
Obverse II 1– *Die marker–* Short vertical die scratch below E in WE.
Reverse B^2c– Doubled bottom edges of top stems and leaves in olives sprig. Doubled bottom of D of DOLLAR, left edge of leg feathers, left edges of first three rays above ONE and left edge of top ray above back of leg feathers. *Die markers–* Short horizontal die scratch at junction of bottom of third ray from bottom of rock. S mint mark set slightly high and slightly to left. Dies clash at fairly early die state.

1925 P

1A1 **II 1 • B^2a (Die Gouge in Rays)** I-3 R-4
Obverse II 1– Horizontal die gouge in rays well below B of LIBERTY.

○1B **II 1 • B^2a (Die Gouge Above IN)** I-2 R-6
Obverse II 1– Three short vertical die gouges above IN.

§1D(revised) **II 1 • B^2a (Die Gouges N-G, Shortened Top Reverse Rays)** I-2 R-5
Obverse B^2a– Vertical die gouges thru left sides of N of IN and G of GOD.
Reverse B^2a– Later die state shows heavy die file lines at top left and right of eagle's shoulders with shortened top left rays away from eagle.

∇1E **II 1 • B^2a (Die Gouge Below R)** I-2 R-5
Obverse II 1– Thin vertical die gouge below R in TRVST.

∇1F **II 1 • B^2a (Die Gouges Below D)** I-2 R-5
Obverse II 1– Three fine vertical gouge lines below D in GOD down to 1 plus shallow broad vertical gouge above top of 1.

#1P **II 1 • B^2a (Die Scratch Left Wing)** I-2 R-5
Reverse B^2a– Long thin and shallow horizontal die scratch at eagle's left wing edge thru second ray from top.

#1Q **II 1 • B^2a (Die Gouges on Cheek, Die File Lines Obverse & Reverse)** I-3 R-5
Obverse II 1– Five horizontal thin shallow die gouges at back of cheek and one gouge in nearby hair. Die file lines in fields.
Reverse B^2a– Die file lines in fields.

#1S **II 1 • B^2a (Die Gouges Below IN G)** I-2 R-5
Obverse II 1– Multiple vertical thin die gouges below IN G.

✚1AA **II 1 • B^2a (Die Gouge Right Side N)** I-2 R-5
Obverse II 1– Vertical shallow die gouge at right side and down at N of IN.

✚1AB **II 1 • B^2a (Rusted/Worn Right Reverse Die)** I-3 R-6
Obverse II 1– Fine die scratch at top of Y in LIBERTY.
Reverse B^2a– Raised dots and splotches mainly in right and top left fields from rusted/worn die.

✚1AD **II 1 • B^2a (Rusted/Worn Obverse Die, Die Gouge R)** I-3 R-6
Obverse II 1– Raised dots and splotches from rusted and worn die on Liberty head and fields. Wide vertical die gouge below R in TRVST.

◊1AE **II 1 • B^2a (Four Die Gouges Above IN)** I-2 R-6
Obverse II 1– Two vertical die gouges above left side of I & N similar to VAMs 1B & 9A. Additional vertical die gouges well above and to left of I and short striated one left of I.

◊1AG **II 1 • B^2a (Die Scratches Face)** I-2 R-5
Obverse II 1– Four diagonal die scratches on Liberty head cheek.

◊1A I **II 1 • B^2a (Die Scratches Left of P, Scribbles at Eagle's Shoulder)** I-2 R-5
Reverse B^2a– Couple diagonal die scratches left of P in PEACE. Scribbling die scratches above and to right of eagle's right shoulder.

♮1AM **II 1 • B^2a (Die Gouge Below T)** I-2 R-5
Obverse II 1– Broad shallow vertical die gouge below left T in TRVST.

♮1AN **II 1 • B^2a (Die Gouge G)** I-2 R-5
Obverse II 1– Vertical die gouge below G in GOD.

✓2A **II 1 • B^2b (Doubled Reverse, Die Gouges Below TR)** I-3 R-5
Obverse II 1– Several shallow thin die gouges below TR in TRVST.

§9A **II 1 • B^2i (Doubled Right Reverse, Die Gouges Above IN)** I-2 R-6
Obverse II 1– Vertical die gouges above I and left side of N plus faint gouge below left side of O in GOD. Similar to VAM 1B but gouge above N is further right and also has gouge below O and lines below date.

§11A **II 1 • B^2k (Doubled Right Leg Feathers, Vertical Die Gouges G & V)** I-2 R-5
Obverse II 1– Vertical die gouge left side of G in GOD and left side of V in TRVST on later die state. (Formerly VAM 1I)

#11B **II 1 • B^2k (Doubled Right Leg Feather, Vertical Die Gouge G & V, File Lines Eagle's Neck)** I-2 R-5
Reverse B^2k– Heavy die file lines thru eagle's neck and on both sides to remove die clash marks.

▸17A **II 1 • B^2p (Doubled Leg Feathers, Die Scratches in Rays & Above Hills)** I-2 R-5
Obverse II 1– Short faint horizontal die scratch in rays above hair left of E.
Reverse B^2p– Thin die gouges between rays above right end of first hill to right of mountain. (Formerly VAM 1G.)

◊18A **II 1 • B^2q (Doubled Lower Edge of Wing, Double Die Gouges Above N)** I-2 R-6
Obverse II 1– Double fine vertical die gouges above N of IN with several fine vertical die scratches above and below IN. (Formerly VAM 1C.)

1925 S

▸1A1 **II 1 • B^2a (Die Gouge Rays Below BE)** I-2 R-5
Obverse II 1– Tiny slanted die gouge in rays below BE in LIBERTY.

•1A2 **II 1 • B²a (Die Gouge Rays Below BE, Die Gouge 2)** **I-2** **R-6**
Obverse II 1– Short shallow die gouge slanted to right from top of 2. Tiny slanted die gouge in rays below BE in LIBERTY.

§1C(revised) **II 1 • B²a (Die Gouges in Rays Between IB and Left of U in UNITED)** **I-2** **R-5**
Obverse II 1– Short shallow diagonal die gouge thru fifth long ray from front.
Reverse B²a– Vertical thin die gouge to left of U in UNITED.

▸1F **II 1 • B²a (Die Gouge Below D)** **I-2** **R-5**
Reverse B²a– Diagonal shallow die gouge from lower left of D in DOLLAR down to tip of top left olive leaf.

1926 P

1 **II 1 • B²a (Normal Die)** **I-1** **R-2**
Obverse II 1– Normal die of II type.
Reverse B²a– Normal die of B² type.

1A **II 1 • B²a (Die Break Edge of Eagle's Wing)** **I-2** **R-6**
Reverse B²a– Die break on the edge of eagle's right wing.

§1B **II 1 • B²a (Shortened Reverse Ray)** **I-2** **R-5**
Reverse B²a– Heavy die file lines at top reverse with shortened second ray from top of eagle's left wing.

§1C1 **II 1 • B²a (Die Gouge Below G)** **I- 2** **R-5**
Obverse II 1– Vertical shallow faint broad die gouge well below G in God.

¶3A **II 2 • B²c (Doubled 6, Die Gouge V)** **I-3** **R-5**
Obverse II 2– Short vertical die gouge below V in TRVST.

¶4A **II 3 • B²a (Doubled Hair, Die Gouge Below V)** **I-2** **R-5**
Obverse II 3– Vertical shallow broad die gouge below V in TRVST and small vertical die gouge below N of IN.

1926 D

✚1C **II 1 • B²a (Die Scratch L)** **I-2** **R-6**
Obverse II 1– Diagonal die scratch above L in LIBERTY.

✗1E **II 1 • B²a (Die Gouge Chin)** **I-2** **R-6**
Obverse II 1– Wide die gouge below Liberty head chin.

1926 S

♯1B1 **II 1 • B²a (Die Gouge Below E)** **I-2** **R-5**
Obverse II 1– Vertical die gouge below E in LIBERTY.

♯1B2 **II 1 • B²a (Die Gouge Below E, Die File Lines Below R)** **I-2** **R-6**
Obverse II 1– Some heavy die file lines below R in LIBERTY and in front of hair bun with weak gouge below E from die file/polishing.

✓1I1(revised) **II 1 • B²a (Double Clash Spikes Eagle's Shoulder)** **I-2** **R-5**
Obverse II 1– *Die marker*– Three horizontal polishing lines thru E in LIBERTY.
Reverse B²a– Die clash double spikes of close spacing up from eagle's right shoulder from back of Liberty head neck on obverse.

✚1N **II 1 • B²a (Die Scratch R)** **I-2** **R-5**
Obverse II 1– Diagonal long die scratch below R in LIBERTY.

✚1Q **II 1 • B²a (Die Gouge B)** **I-2** **R-5**
Obverse II 1– Vertical short die gouge at first short ray to right of B in LIBERTY.

✗ 1S **II 1 • B²a (Die Gouges R)** **I-2** **R-5**
Obverse II 1– Die file lines with vertical die gouges below R in LIBERTY.

♮1U **II 1 • B²a (Die Gouges B & R)** **I-2** **R-5**
Obverse II 1– Slightly shallow die gouges at left of B and thru R in LIBERTY.

♮1V **II 1 • B²a (Die Gouge B)** **I-2** **R-5**
Obverse II 1– Vertical shallow die gouges at left side of B in LIBERTY.

♮1W **II 1 • B²a (Die Gouges Below Y)** **I-2** **R-5**
Obverse II 1– Several shallow vertical die gouges below Y in LIBERTY.

♮1Y **II 1 • B²a (Die Gouge I)** **I-2** **R-5**
Obverse II 1– Vertical striated die gouge thru I in LIBERTY.

∇2A **II 1 • B²b (High S, Comet Die Gouge)** **I-3** **R-5**
Obverse II 1– Oblong, broad die gouge in shape of a comet below R in LIBERTY with die file lines around it.

1927 D

♯3A **II 3 • B²a (Doubled Left Obverse, Die Gouge Below E)** **I-3** **R-6**
Obverse II 3– Two striated diagonal die gouge in rays below E and to left of E in LIBERTY. (Formerly VAM 1A)

1927 S

◇1I **II 1 • B²a (Gouges Hair Bun)** **I-3** **R-6**
Obverse II 1– Several smooth top die gouges at top of hair bun. Slightly beveled field at hair front.

1934 P

¶1A **III 1 • B²a (Semi-circular Die Scratch Obverse)** **I-2** **R-5**
Obverse III 1– Long thin semi-circular die scratch from L in LIBERTY down thru G in GOD over to Liberty head neck point.

◇1D **III 1 • B²a (Die Gouge Rim at I)** **I-2** **R-5**
Obverse III 1– Broken die gouge near rim to right of I in LIBERTY. Some die file lines in fields and circular depression above W in WE from possible die impression.

✗1F **III 1 • B²a (Lines in O)** **I-2** **R-5**
Obverse III 1– Four vertical lines with end loops from possible die scratches or thread impression inside O of GOD.

1934 D

✚1C **III²1 • B²a (Micro D, Die Scratch Below D)** **I-2** **R-5**
Obverse III²1– Thin shallow long vertical die scratch below D of GOD and short scratch below left side of G.

§2A **III 1 • B²b (Medium D, Die Gouge Below G)** **I-2** **R-5**
Obverse III 1– Vertical shallow die gouge below G in GOD.

1935 P

#1A(revised) **III 1 • B^2a (Die Scratches Right Reverse)** **I-3** **R-5**

Reverse B^2a– Thin horizontal die scratches above middle olive leaves, in rays above R in DOLLAR and across ray below eagle's right shoulder.

¤1B1 **III 1 • B^2a (Die Scratch to Right of Middle Olive Leaves)** **I-2** **R-5**

Reverse B^2a– Thin horizontal die scratch to right of middle olive leaves.

✚1B2 **III 1 • B^2a (Die Scratch Right of Middle Olive Leaves, Die Gouges T)** **I-2** **R-6**

Obverse III 1– Short shallow vertical die gouges above and below left T in TRVST.

§1C **III 1 • B^2a (Die Scratch Reverse Top Ray)** **I-2** **R-5**

Reverse B^2a– Thin horizontal die scratch thru top of ray to right of eagle's neck.

1935 S

♮3B **III 1 • Ca (Die Gouge R)** **I-2** **R-5**

Obverse III 1– Vertical die gouge right of R and vertical die scratch right of B in LIBERTY.

§5A **III 1 • B^2c (Doubled Reverse Left Rays, Die Gouge Below Olive Leaves)** **I-2** **R-5**

Reverse B^2c– Horizontal die gouge below olive leaves.

PHOTOGRAPHS OF DIE GOUGES AND SCRATCHES
APPENDIX A: Feed Fingers Die Gouges

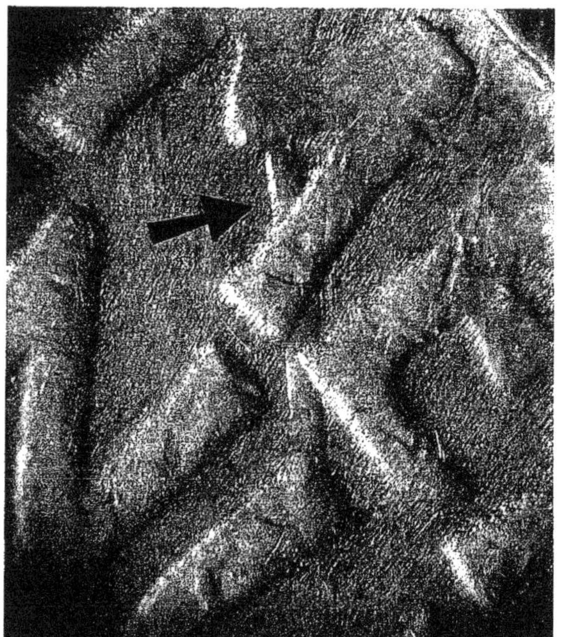
1921 Peace VAM 1E2 Die Gouge ME

1921 Peace VAM 1J Die Gouge ME

1922 P VAM 1B Bar Die Gouge G

1922 P VAM 1D Die Gouge Between N-G

1922 P VAM 1H Gouge Bar Between N-G

1922 P VAM 1P Double Die Gouges Below G

Feed Fingers Die Gouges

1922 P VAM 1Q Die Gouge Below N-G

1922 P VAM 2E Vertical Die Gouge 19

1922 P VAM 2J Bar R Die Gouge

1922 P VAM 1U Die Gouge Below VS

1922 P VAM 2F Die Gouge Below R

1922 P VAM 2M Die Gouge Between GO

Feed Fingers Die Gouges

1922 P VAM 2P Chin Bar Die Gouge

1922 P VAM 2R Die Gouge GO

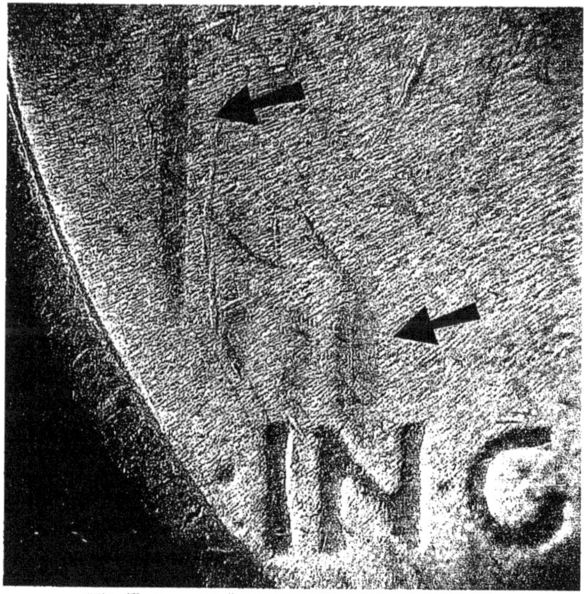

1922 P VAM 2S Triple Die Gouges

1922 P VAM 2W Die Gouge Left of G

1922 P VAM 2Z Vertical Die Gouge N

1922 P VAM 2AX Die Gouge G

1922 P VAM 2BL Die Scratches S

1922 P VAM 2CC Die Gouges Below RV

1922 P VAM 2CQ Die Gouges Below G

1922 P VAM 2CR Die Gouge G Left

1922 P VAM 2CU Die Scratches OD

1922 P VAM 2CW Die Gouges Below OD

Feed Fingers Die Gouges

1922 P VAM 2DD Die Gouge Below In

1922 P VAM 2DE Die Gouges/Scratches GOD

1922 P VAM 2DM Die Gouge IN

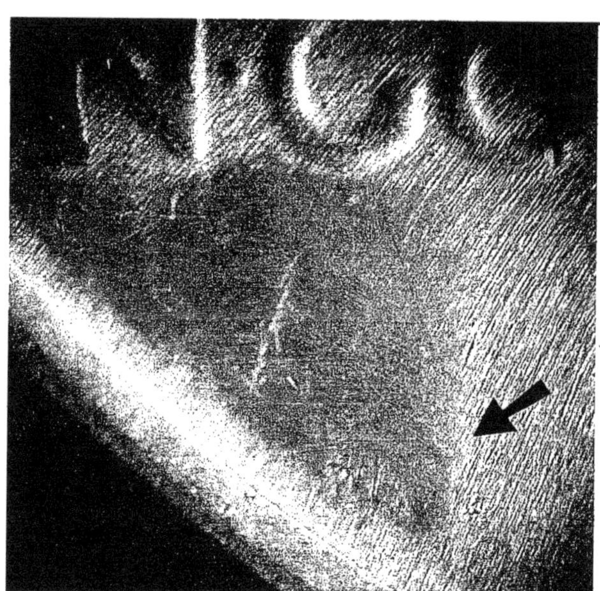

1922 P VAM 2DQ Die Gouge Below GO

1922 P VAM 5-2 Die Gouge G

1922 P VAM 5A1 Die Gouge G

Feed Fingers Die Gouges

1922 P VAM 5C Die Gouge G

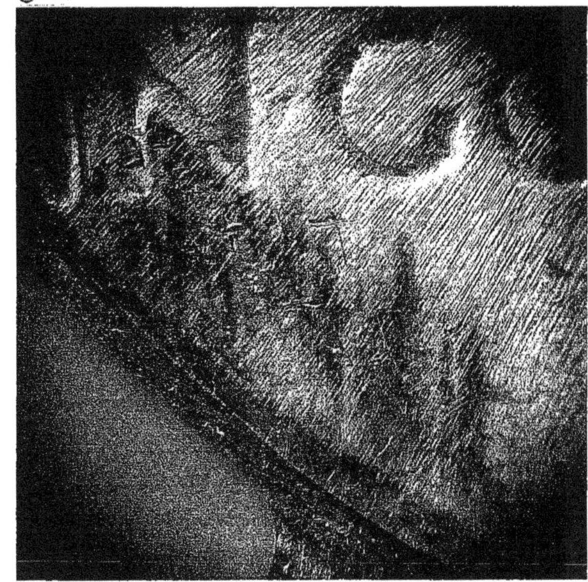
1922 P VAM 25A Die Gouges Below IN-G

1922 P VAM 29A Die Gouges Below IN

1922 P VAM 31A Die Gouges Above IN

1922 P VAM 34A Die Gouges Right 2

1922 P VAM 54A Die Gouge N

1922 D VAM 2W Bar N Die Gouge

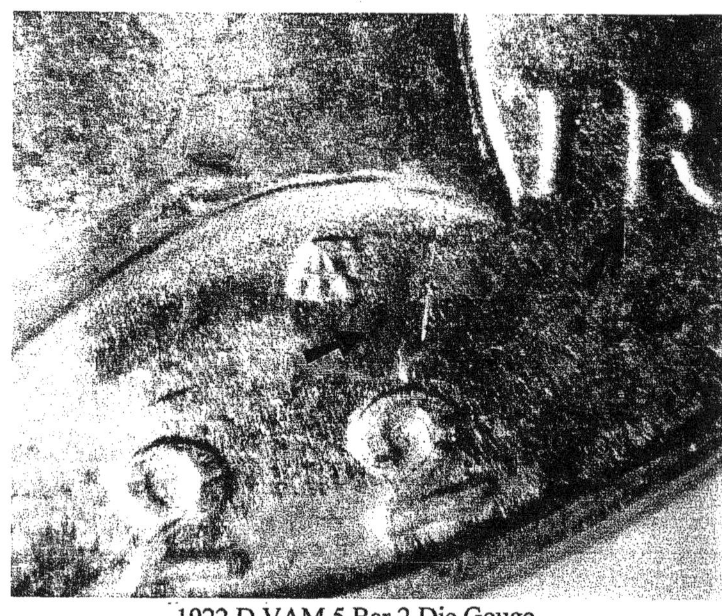
1922 D VAM 5 Bar 2 Die Gouge

1922 S VAM 1A Die Gouge I

1922 S VAM 2AI Die Gouges Front Rays

1923 P VAM 1C Bar S Die Gouge

1923 P VAM 1F1 Chin Bar Die Gouge

1923 P VAM 1G Die Gouge O

1923 P VAM 1N Die Gouges G & D

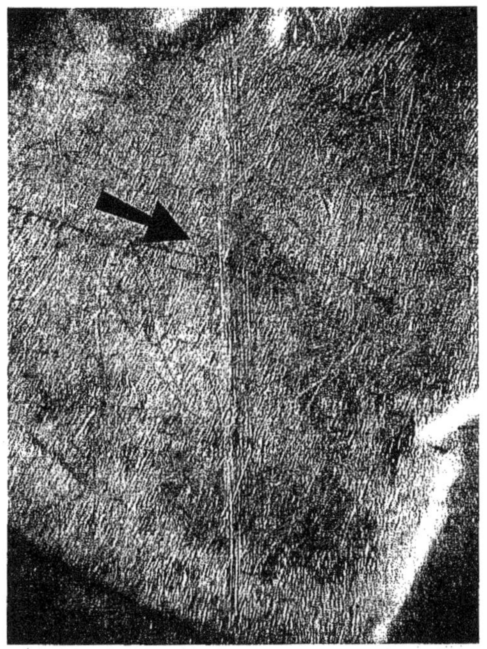

1923 P VAM 1U Die Gouge Below O

1923 P VAM 1X Bar S Die Gouge

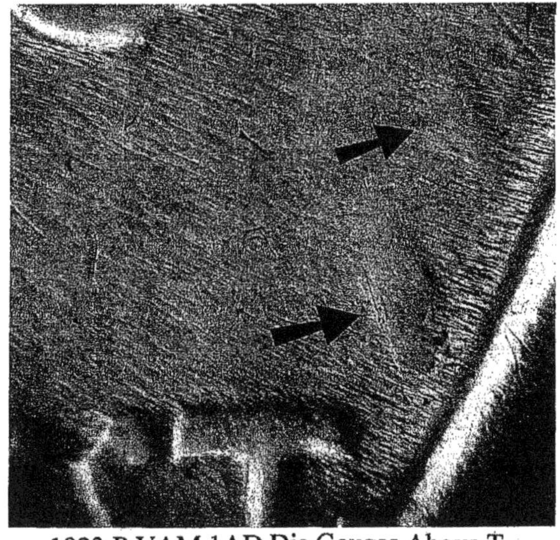

1923 P VAM 1AD Die Gouges Above T

1923 P VAM 1AI Die Gouge T

1923 P VAM 1AS Die Gouge Thru RV

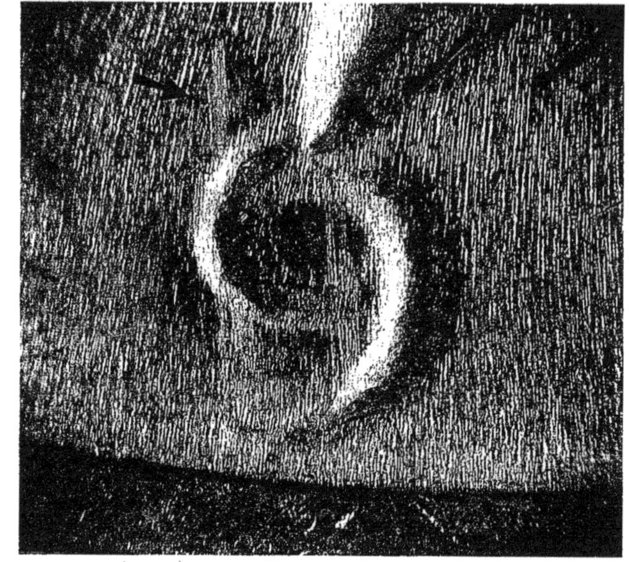

1923 P VAM 1BA Die Gouges 9

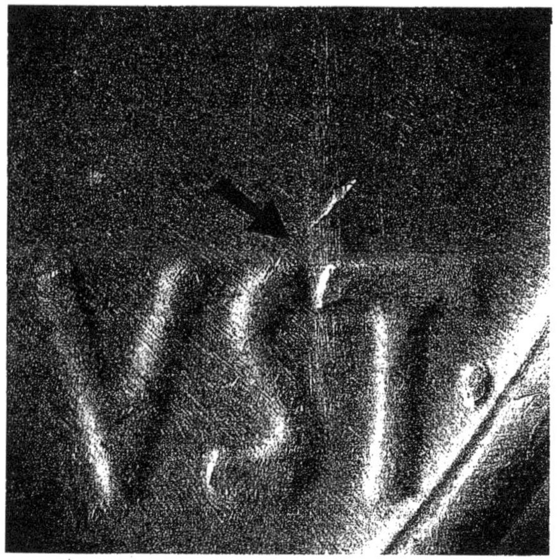

1923 P VAM 1BF Die Gouge Right T

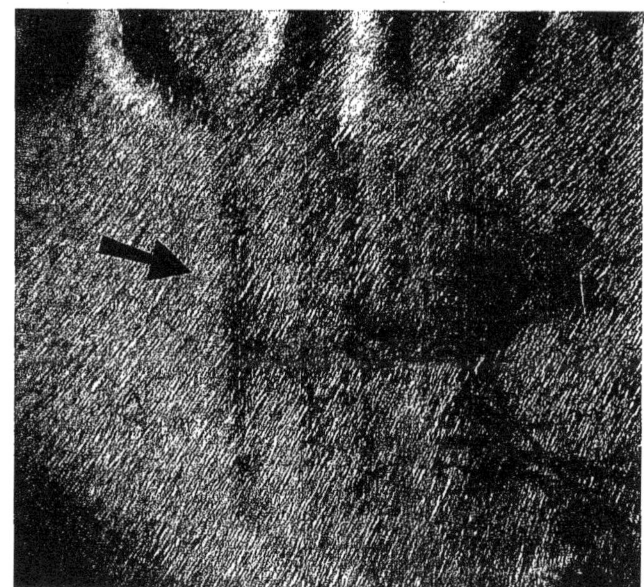

1923 P VAM 1BM Die Gouges Below OD

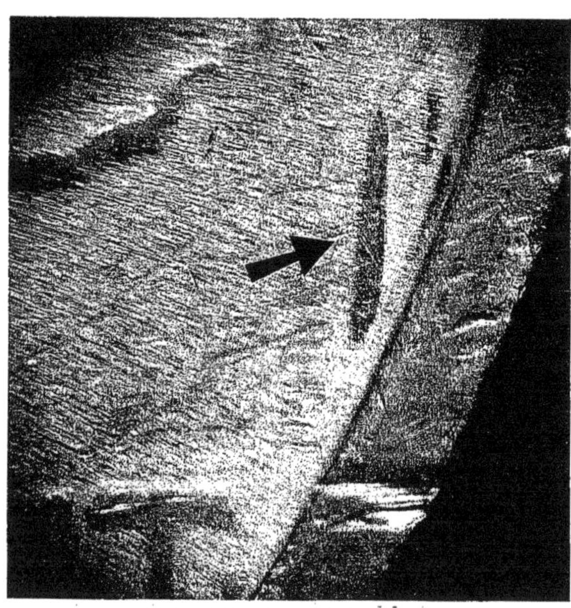

1923 P VAM 1BO Triple Die Gouges

1923 P VAM 1BR Striated Die Gouge Above N

1923 P VAM 1BT Die Gouge RV

1923 P VAM 1BY Polished Gouge Triangle 19

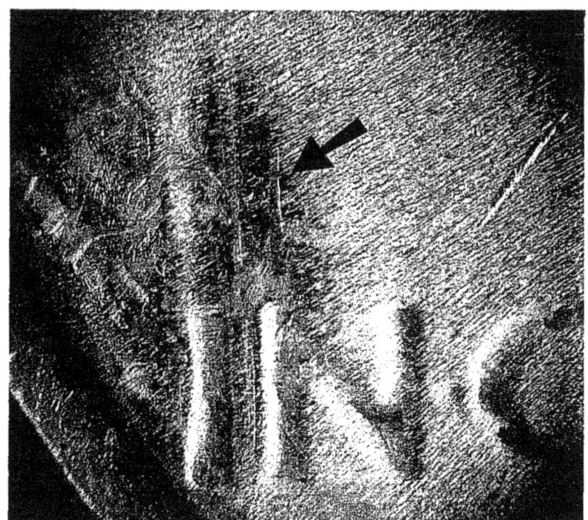
1923 P VAM 1CB Die Gouges Above IN

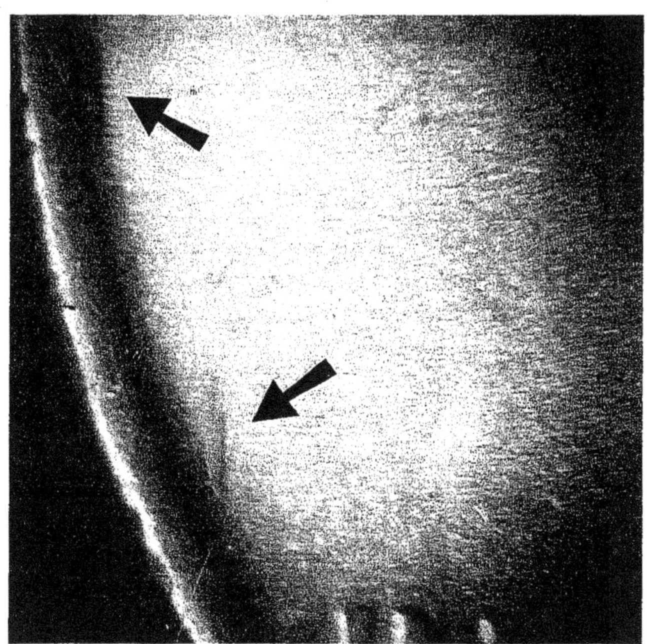
1923 P VAM 1CC Die Gouges Left Rim

1923 P VAM 1CH Short Die Gouges Below N & G

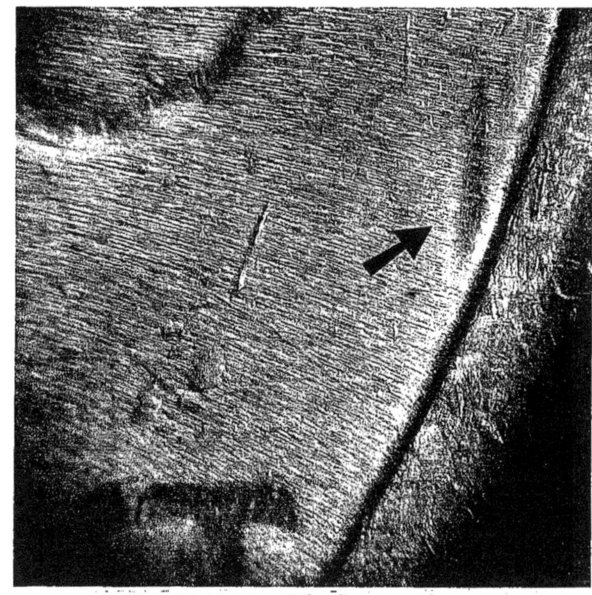
1923 P VAM 7A Die Gouge Above T

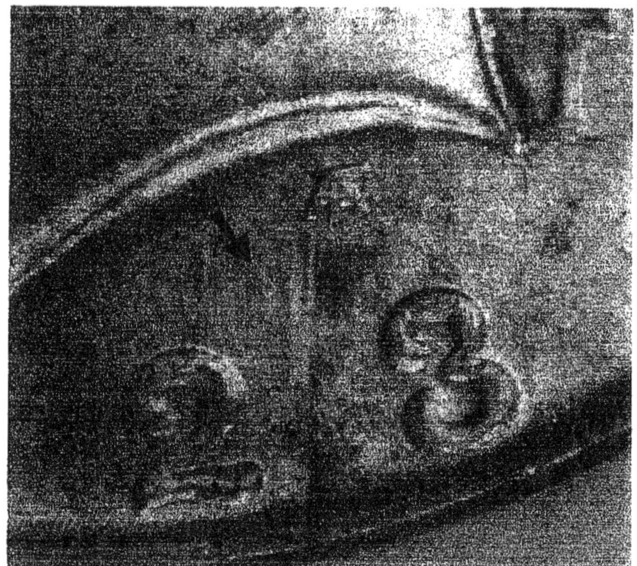
1923 D VAM 1D Die Gouge Below Neck

1923 D VAM 1AG Polished Areas With Scratches

1923 D VAM 1AX1 Die Gouge Below WE

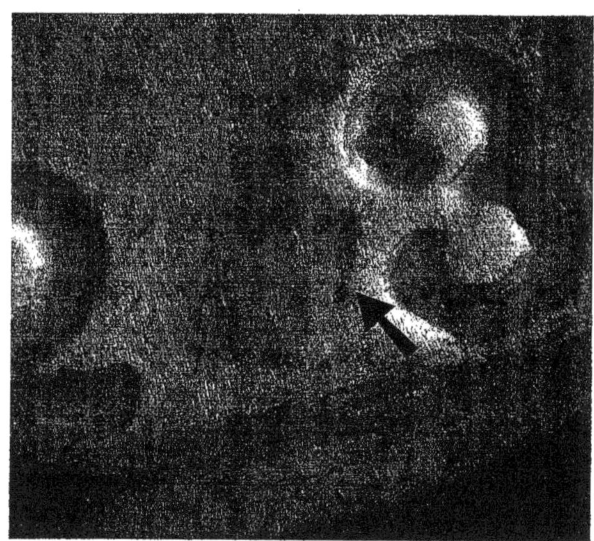
1923 D VAM 1BI Die Gouge 3

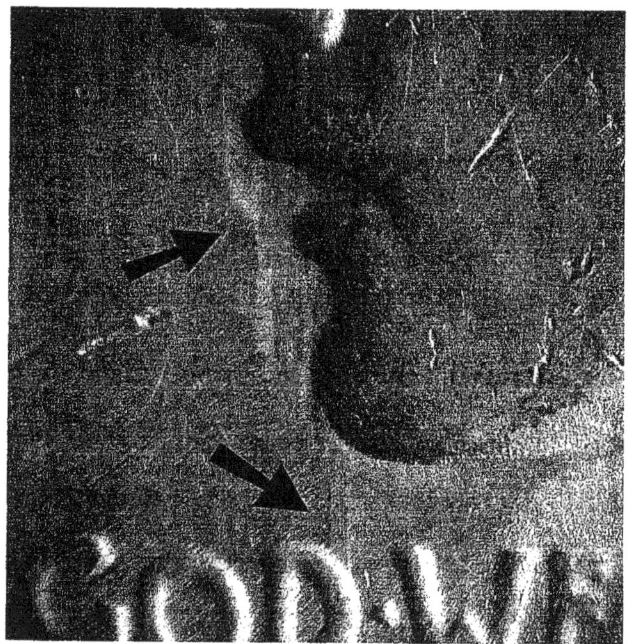
1923 D VAM 1BK Die Gouge Chin

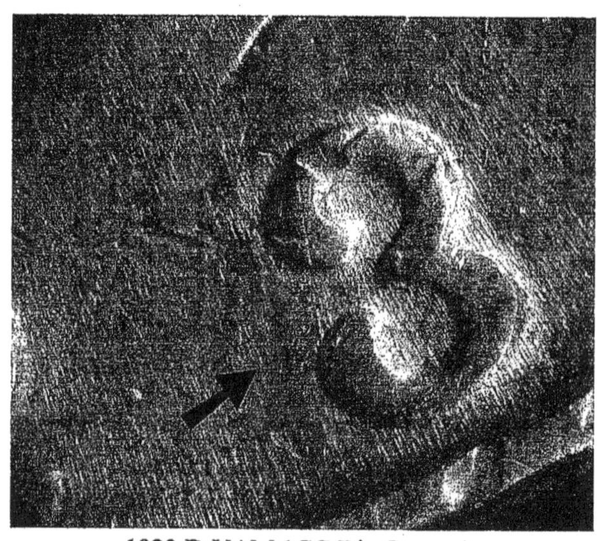
1923 D VAM 1CC Die Gouge 3

Feed Fingers Die Gouges

1923 D VAM 1CE Die Gouge Scraped Bars

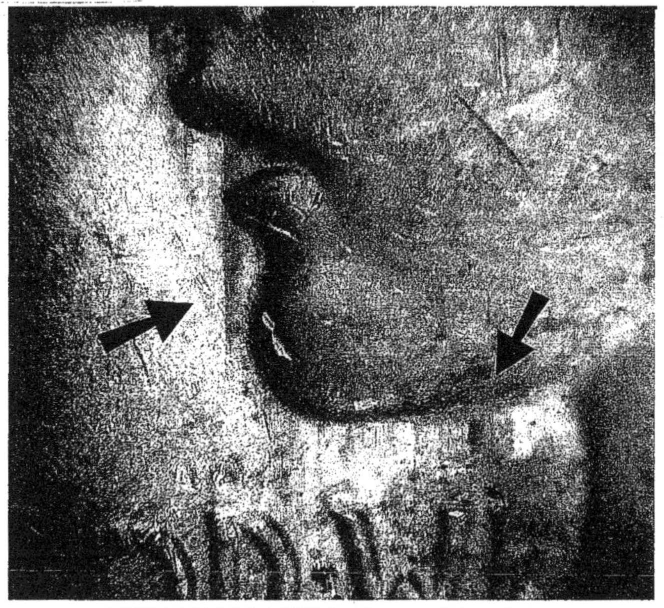

1923 D VAM 1CF Die Gouges Lips & Jaw

1923 S VAM 1BX Die Gouge Rays

1923 S VAM 1CP Die Gouge Ray B

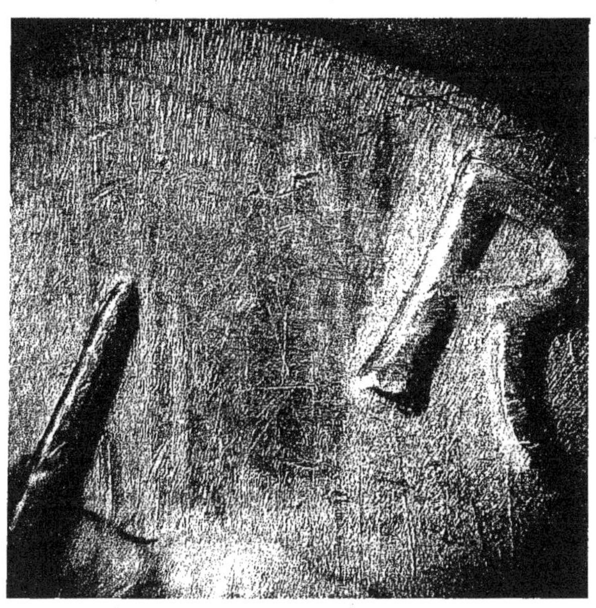

1923 S VAM 1CR Die Gouges ER

1924 P VAM 1A1 Bar D Die Gouge

Feed Fingers Die Gouges

1924 P VAM 1E Die Gouge G

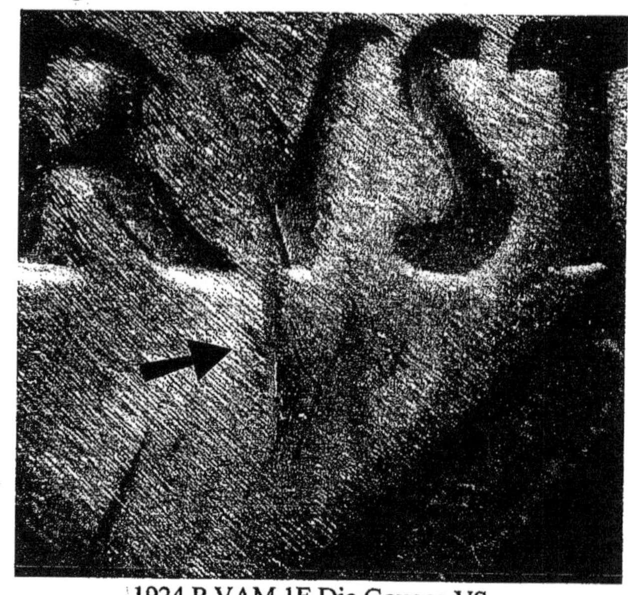
1924 P VAM 1F Die Gouges VS

1924 P VAM 1K1 Die Gouge Left Side G

1924 P VAM 1L Die Gouge Left of G

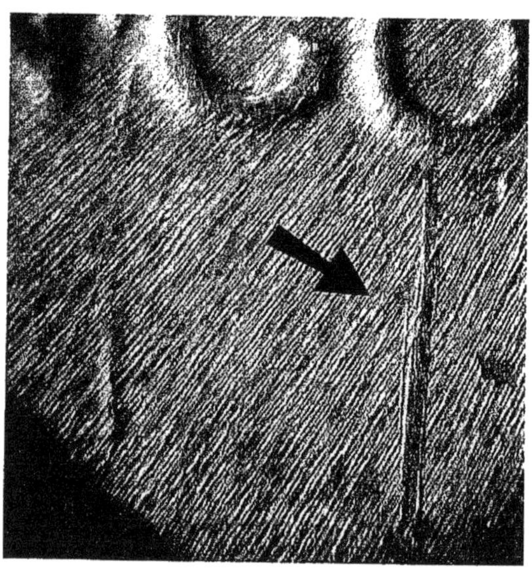
1924 P VAM 1M Die Gouge GO

1924 P VAM 1N Die Gouge S

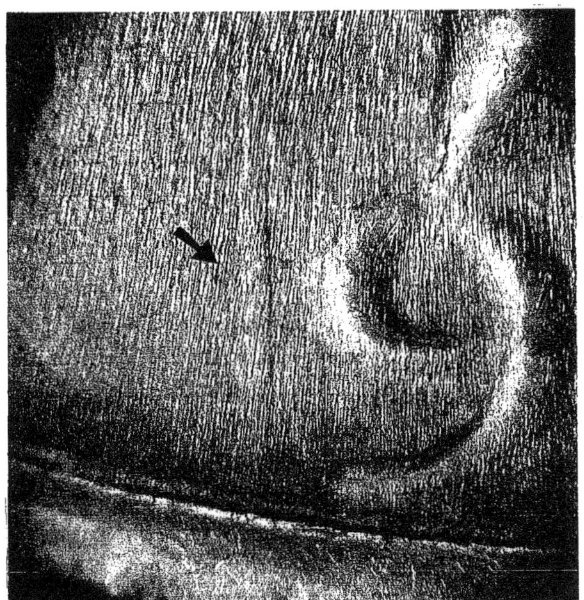
1924 P VAM 1 O Die Gouge Between 19

1924 P VAM 1S Die Gouge Between O-D

1924 P VAM 1U Die Gouge Below N

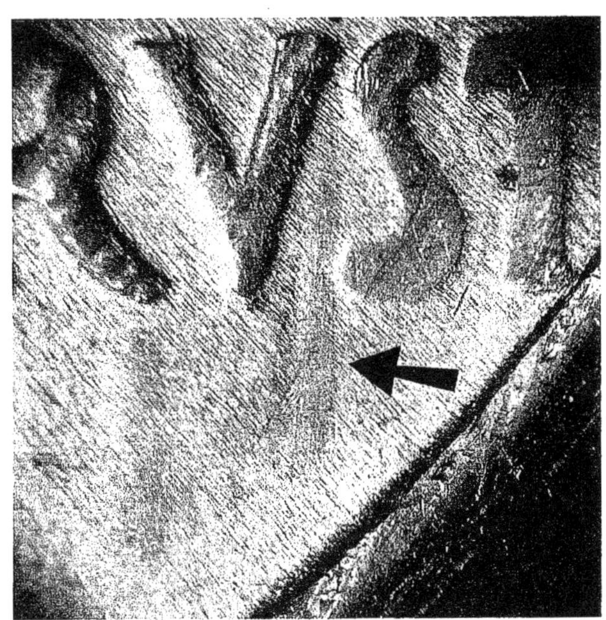
1924 P VAM 1Y Die Gouge VS

1924 P VAM 1Z Die Gouge Rt. Of G

1924 P VAM 1AI Die Gouges VS

Feed Fingers Die Gouges

1924 P VAM 1AJ Die Gouges S

1924 P VAM 1AL Triple Die Gouges Below G

1924 P VAM 1AR Die Gouge 24

1924 P VAM 1AU Die Gouge O

1924 P VAM 1AV Die Gouge N

1924 P VAM 1BT Die Gouge RV

1925 P VAM 1B Die Gouges Above IN

1925 P VAM 1D Die Gouges N-G

1925 P VAM 1E Die Gouge Below R

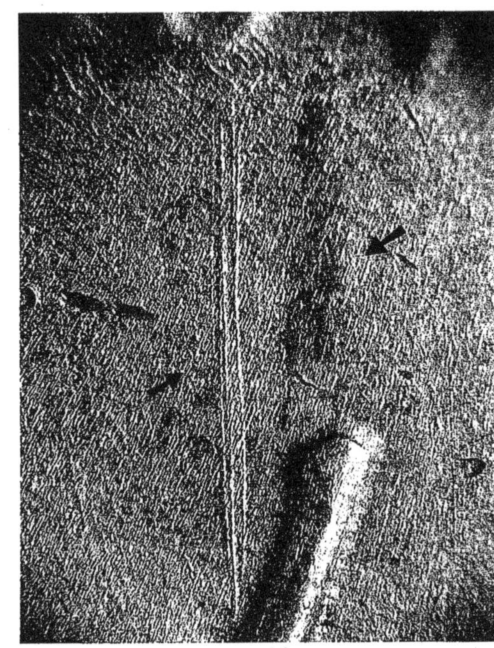

1925 P VAM 1F Die Gouges Below D

1925 P VAM 1S Die Gouge Below IN G

1925 P VAM 1AA Die Gouge Right Side N

1925 P VAM 1AD Die Gouge R

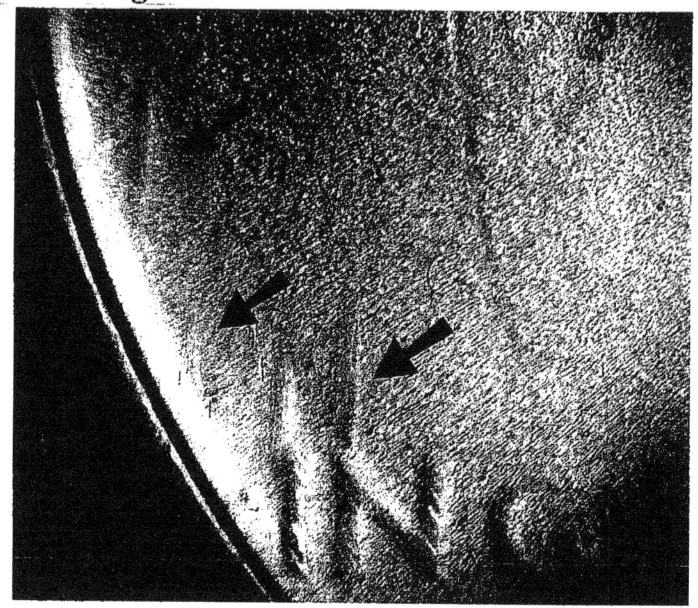
1925 P VAM 1AE Four Die Gouges Above IN

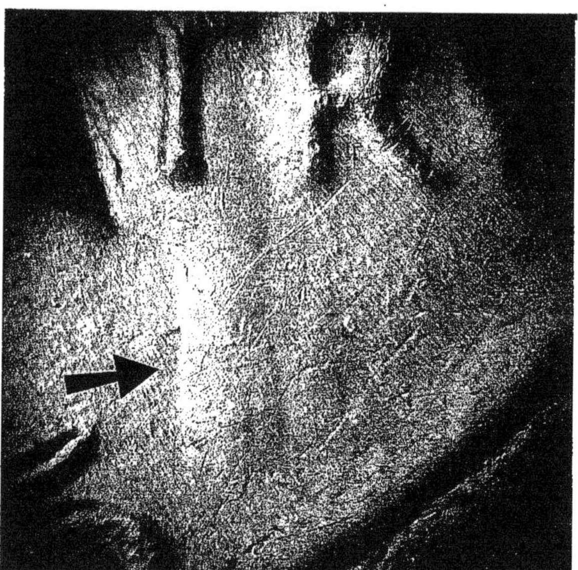
1925 P VAM 1AM Die Gouge T

1925 P VAM 1AN Die Gouge Below G

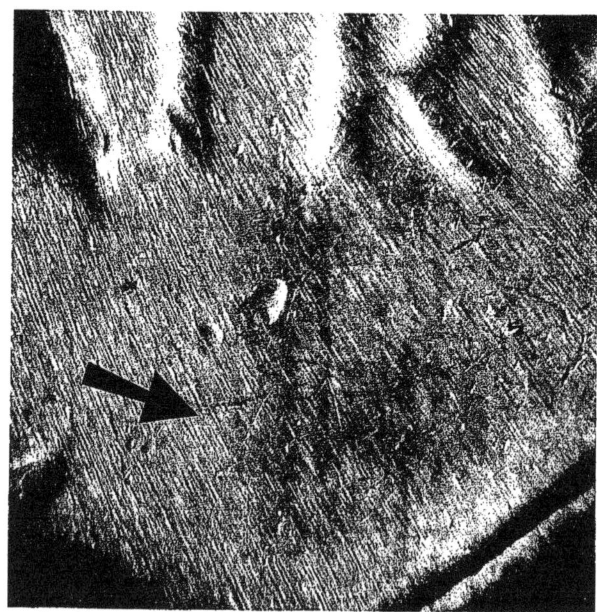
1925 P VAM 2A Die Gouges Below TR

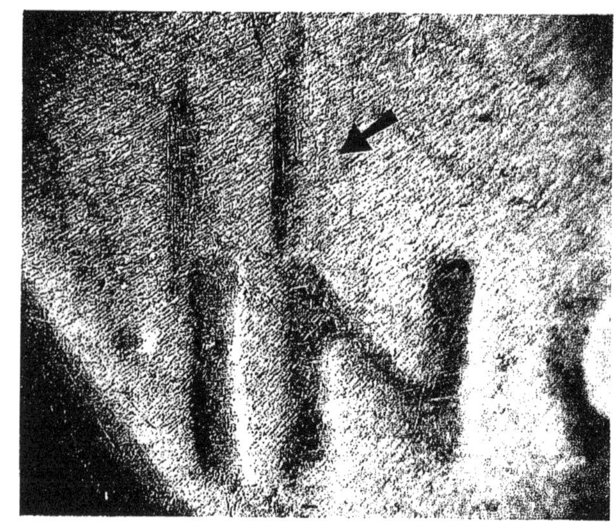
1925 P VAM 9A Die Gouges Above IN

1925 P VAM 11A Die Gouge G

1925 P VAM 18A Die Gouges N

1926 P VAM 1C1 Die Gouge Below G

1926 P VAM 3A Die Gouge V

1926 P VAM 4A Die Gouge Below V

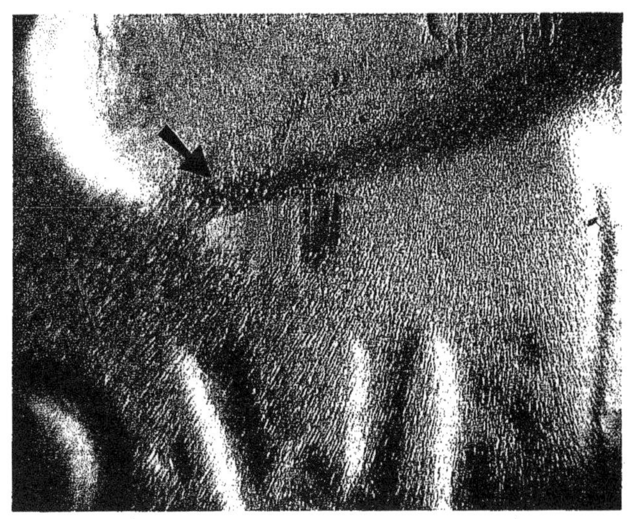

1926 D VAM 1E Die Gouge Chin

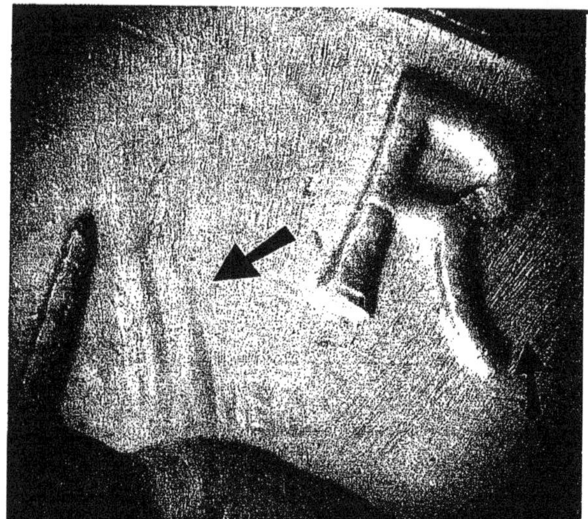
1926 S VAM 1S Die Gouges R

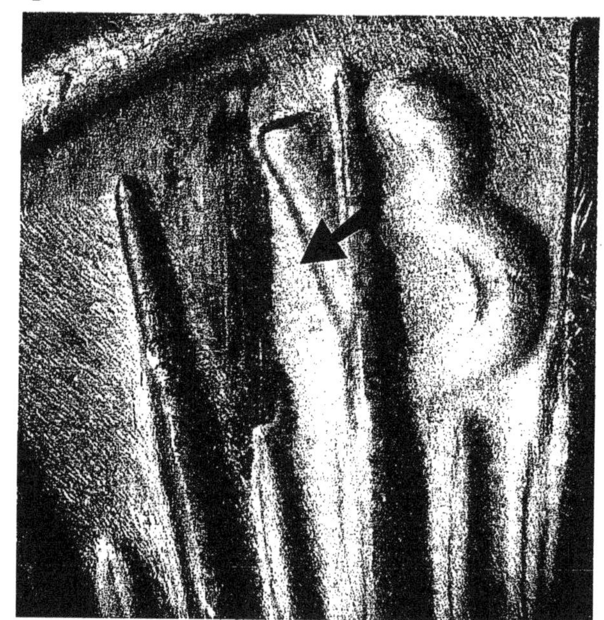
1926 S VAM 1U Die Gouge B

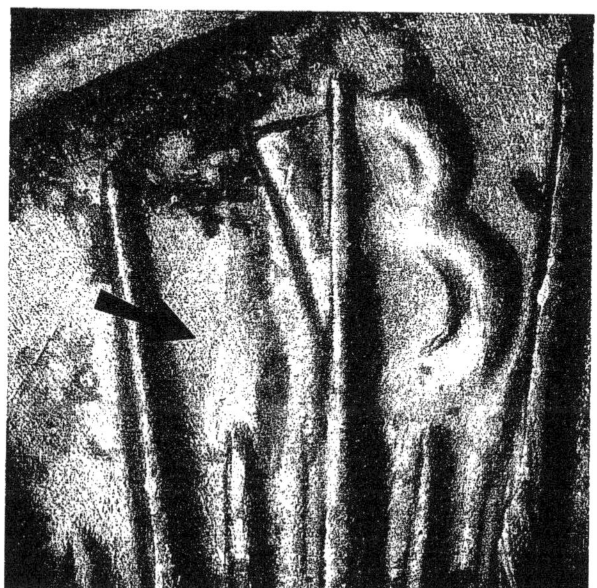
1926 S VAM 1V Die Gouge B

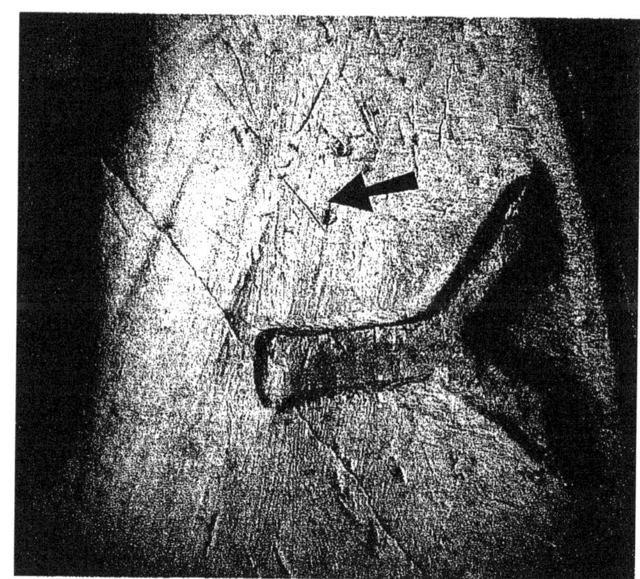
1926 S VAM 1W Die Gouges Y

1926 S VAM 1Y Die Gouge I

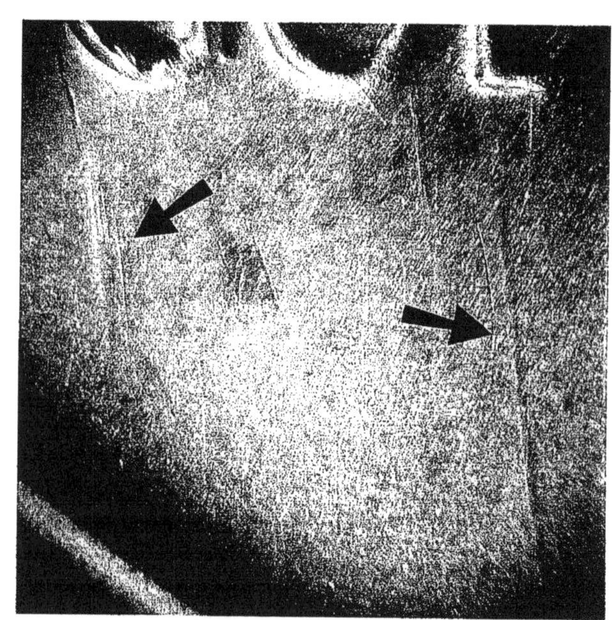
1934 D VAM 1C Die Gouges Below G-D

1934 D VAM 2A Die Gouge Below G

1935 S VAM 3B Die Gouge R

APPENDIX B: Die Edge Gouges on Obverse

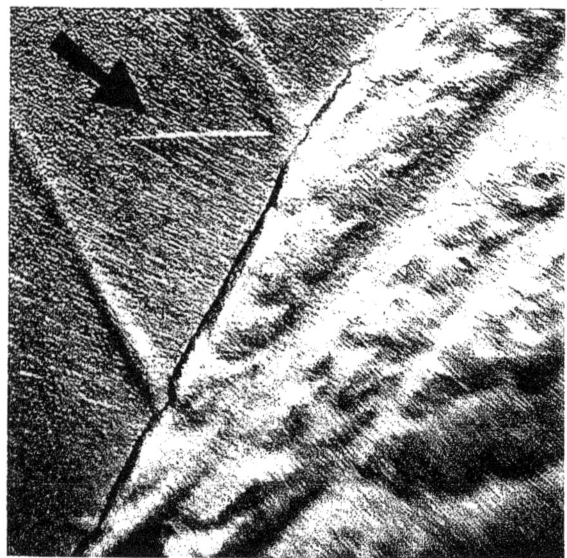

1921 Peace VAM 1E Die Edge Gouges Left Field

1921 Peace VAM 1T Die Scratch Thru RICA

1921 Peace VAM 1X Die Edge Gouge Spiked Eagle

1922 P VAM 1A Die Edge Gouge Rays

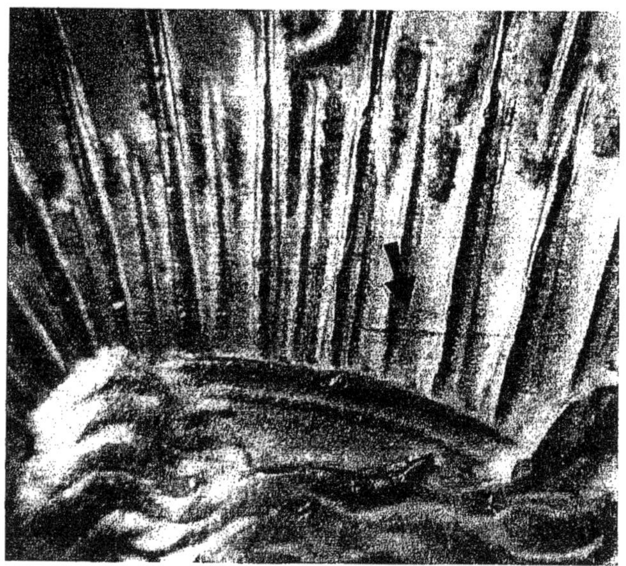

1922 P VAM 1C Die Edge Gouge Rays

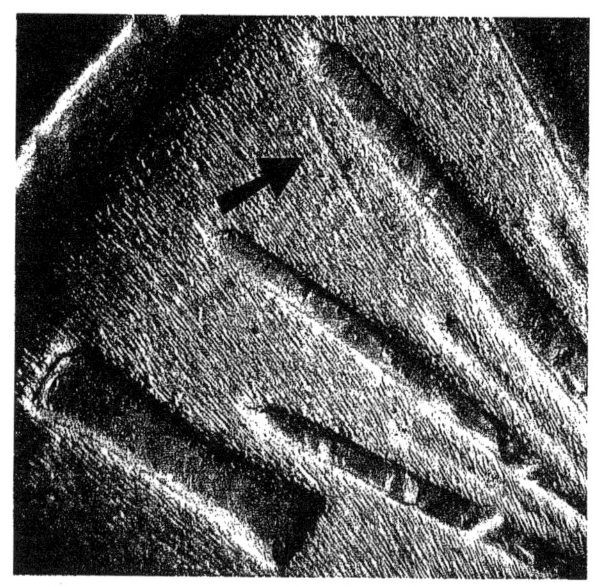

1922 P VAM 1X Die Edge Scratch Ray

1922 P VAM 2F Die Edge Gouge Below E

1922 P VAM 2H Die Edge Gouge Below B

1922 P VAM 2K Die Edge Gouge Between B-E

1922 P VAM 2X Diagonal Die Edge Gouge 2

1922 P VAM 2Y Diagonal Die Edge Gouge Y

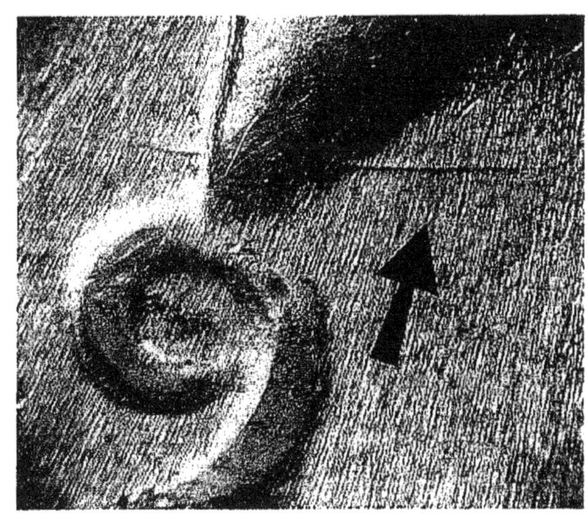
1922 P VAM 1AC Spiked Neck Die Edge Gouge

1922 P VAM 2AI Die Edges Gouges Between ER

1922 P VAM 2AK Die Edge Gouge Last Ray

1922 P VAM 2AL Die Edge Gouge Rays Below E

1922 P VAM 2AR Die Edge Scratch Ray

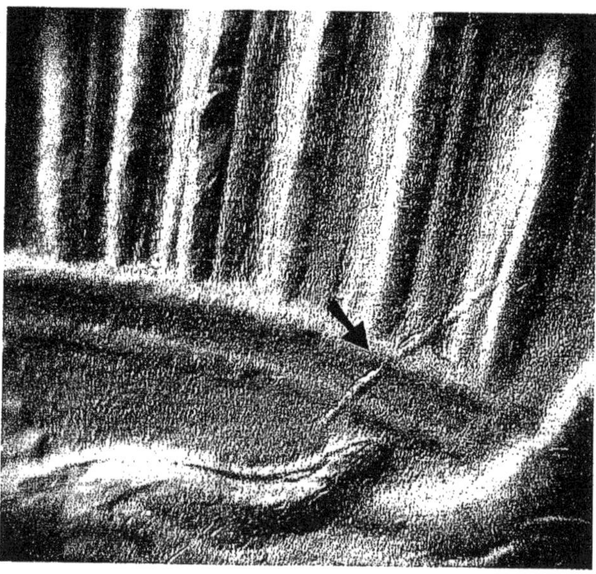
1922 P VAM 2AW Die Edge Scratch Headband

1922 P VAM 2BJ Shallow Die Edge Gouge

1922 P VAM BO Die Edge Gouge Hair Strands

1922 P VAM 1BQ Die Edge Scratch WE

1922 P VAM 2DG Die Edge Gouges Cheek

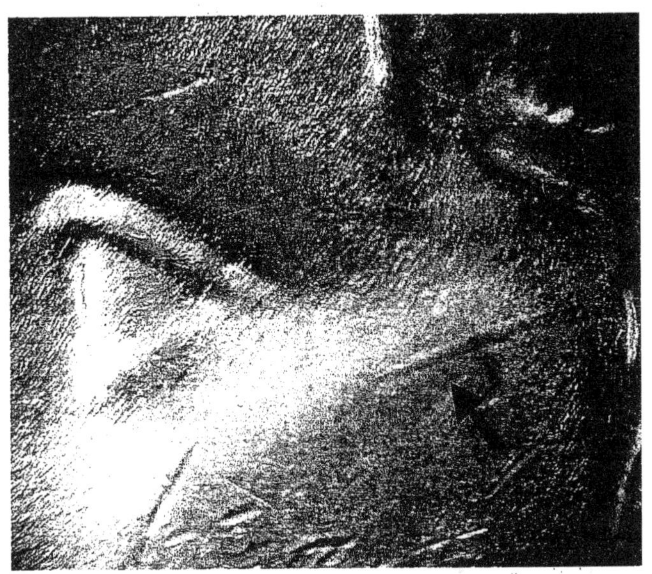

1922 P VAM 2DQ Die Edge Gouge Eye

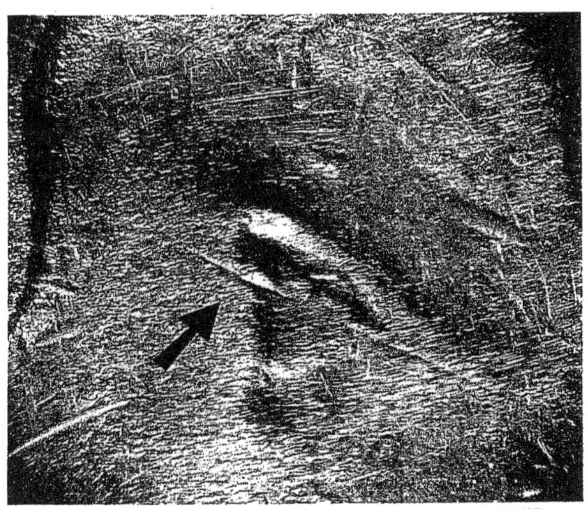

1922 D VAM 1F Spiked Eye Die Edge Gouge

1922 D VAM 1P Shallow Die Edge Gouge IE

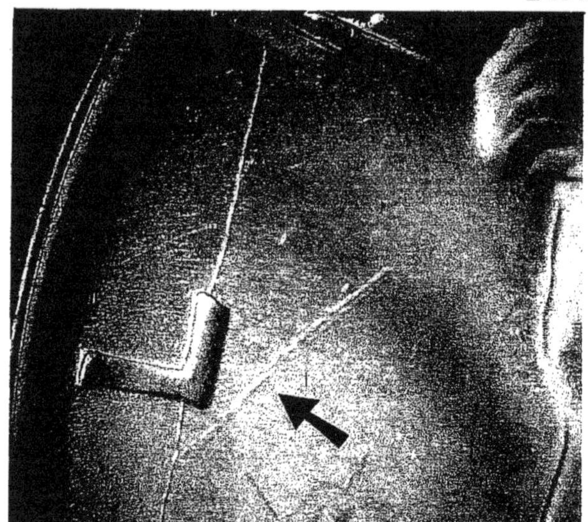

1922 D VAM 2BJ Die Edge Gouge L

1922 D VAM 2BO Die Edge Gouge Below G

1922 D VAM 7 Die Edge Gouge Tiara

1922 S VAM 2I Die Edge Scratch W

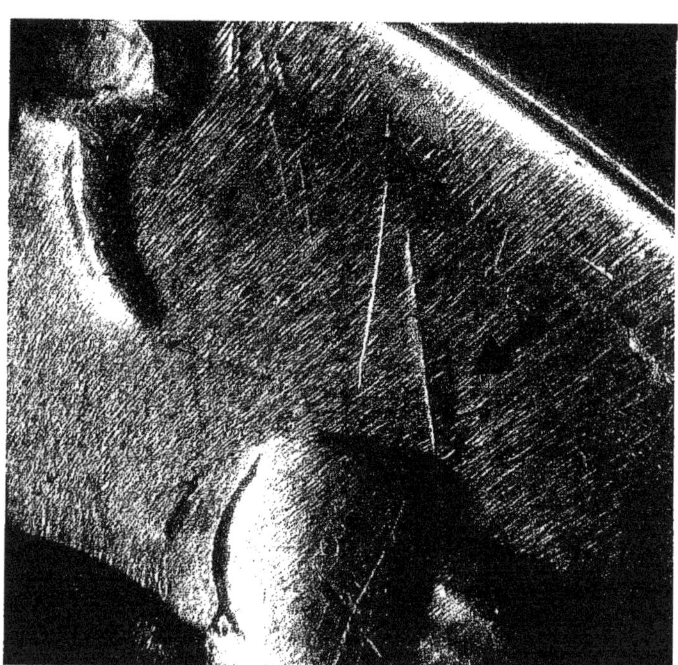

1922 S VAM 2Z Die Edge Scratch Hair Bun

1922 S VAM 5A Die Edge Scratch Above 2

1923 P VAM 1G Die Edge Gouge Below B

1923 P VAM 1J Die Edge Gouge Front Rays

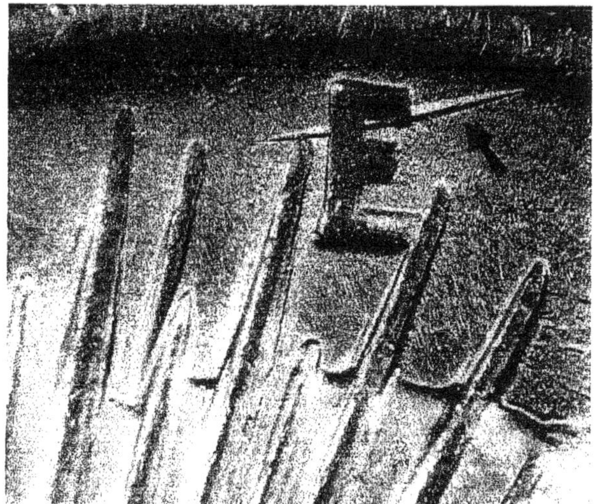
1923 P VAM 1K Die Edge Gouge E

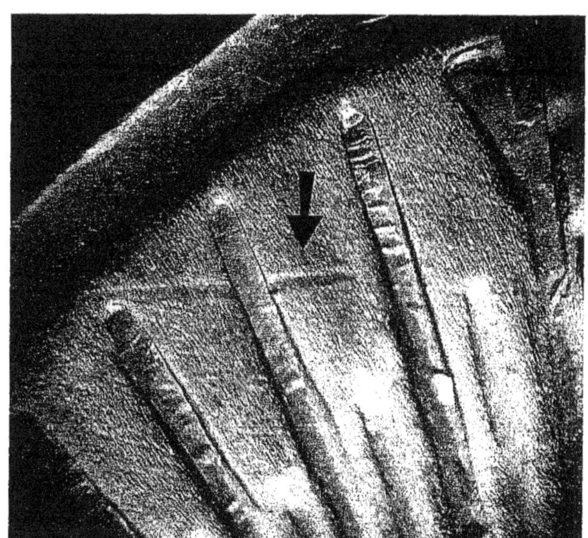
1923 P VAM 1L1 Die Edge Gouge Front Long Ray

1923 P VAM 1M Die Edge Gouge Rays

1923 P VAM 1P Die Edge Gouge R

1923 P VAM 1R Die Edge Gouge Upper Hair

1923 P VAM 1AG Diagonal Die Edge Scratch O

1923 P VAM 1AM Die Edge Scratches 1

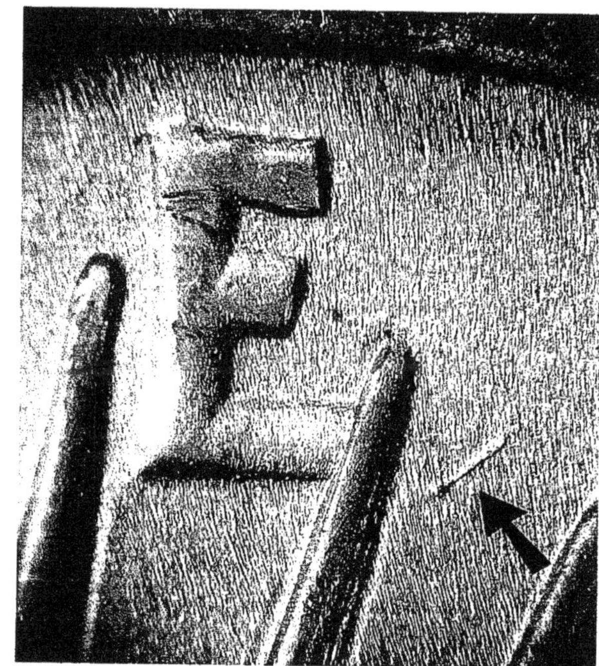
1923 P VAM 1AO Die Edge Gouge Rt. Of E

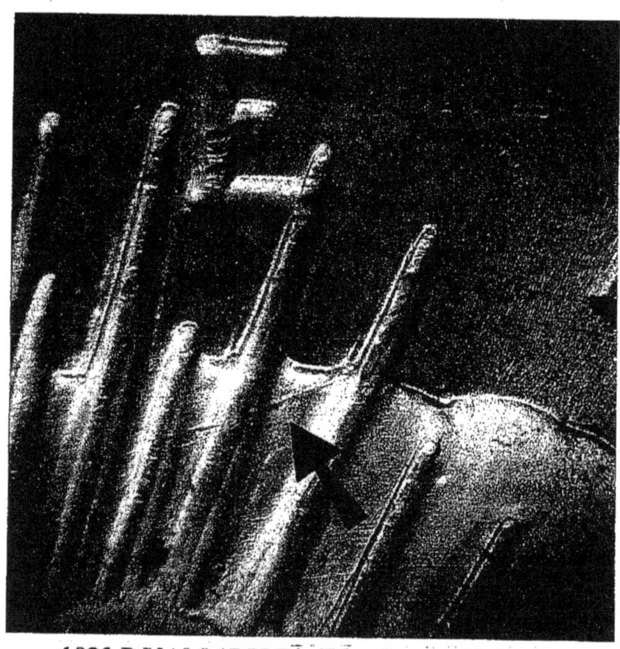
1923 P VAM 1BH Die Edge Scratch Below E

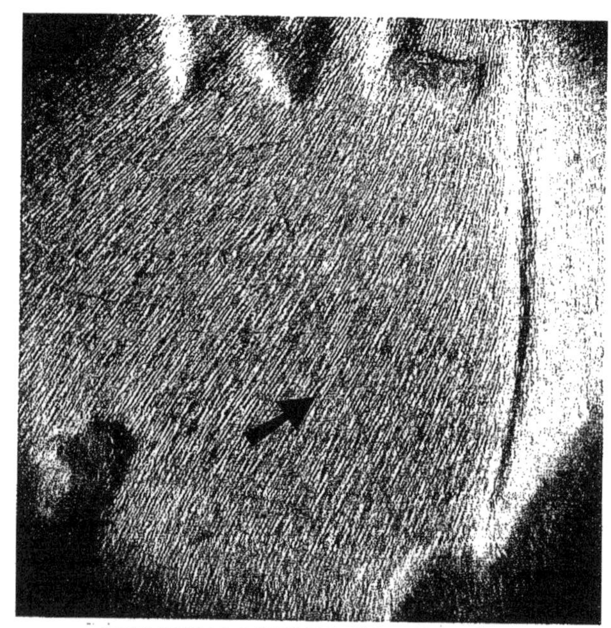
1923 P VAM 1BS Die Edge Scratch 9

1923 D VAM 1V Die Edge Gouge Below B

1923 D VAM 1AN Die Edge Scratch Ray

1923 S VAM 1O Short Die Edge Gouge Ray

1923 S VAM 1BW Die Edge Scratches Rear Rays

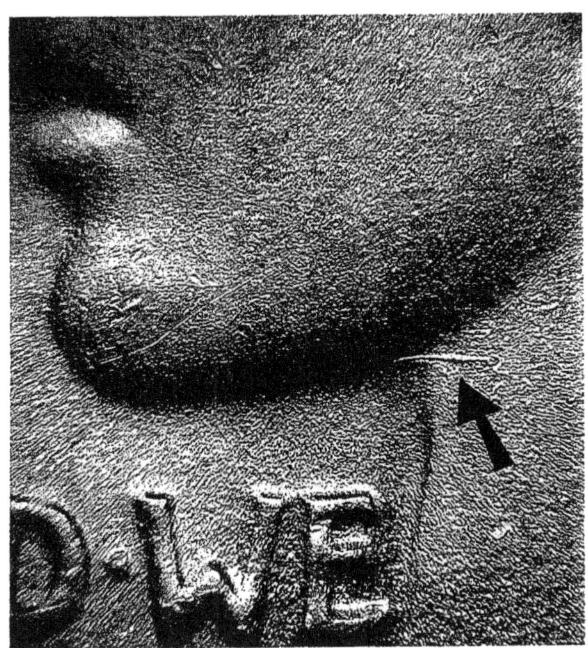

1924 P VAM 1AD Cut Throat Die Edge Scratch

1924 P VAM 1AS Die Edge Scratch 9

Die Edge Gouges, Obverse

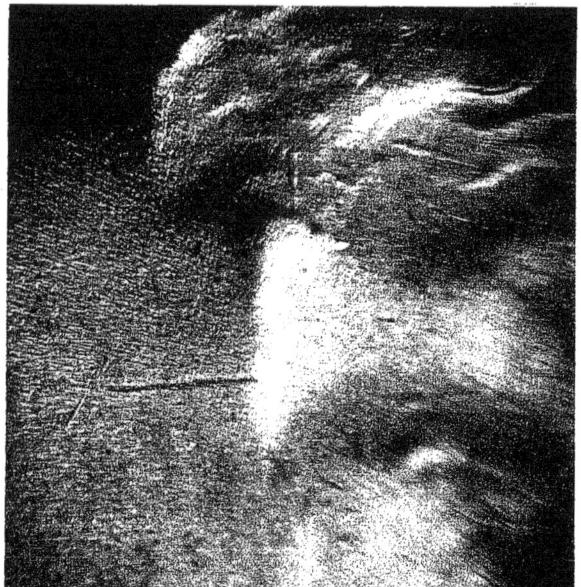
1924 P VAM 1AT Spiked Forehead Die Edge Scratch

1924 P VAM 1AY Die Edge Scratch Behind Rays

1924 P VAM 1BE Die Edge Scratches Face

1924 P VAM 8B Die Edge Gouge Eye

1924 S VAM 1C Die Edge Scratch T

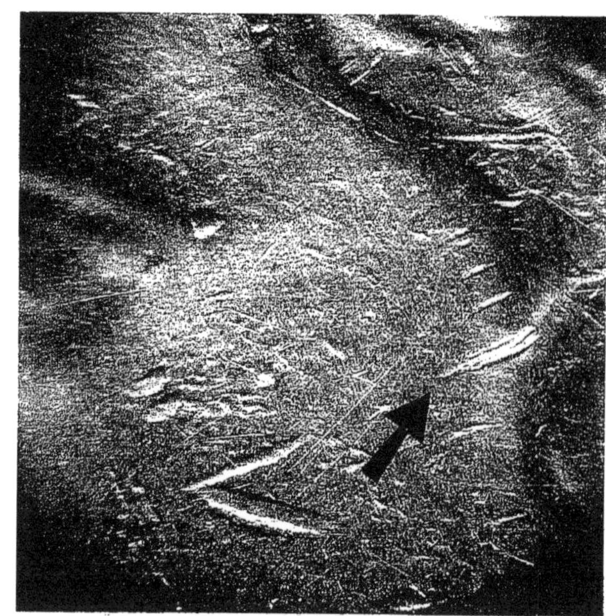
1924 S VAM 1L Die Edge Gouges Hair Edge

1925 P VAM 1A Die Edge Gouge Rays

1925 P VAM 1AB Die Edge Scratch Y

1925 S VAM 1A1 Die Edge Gouge Rays

1925 S VAM 1A2 Die Edge Gouge 2

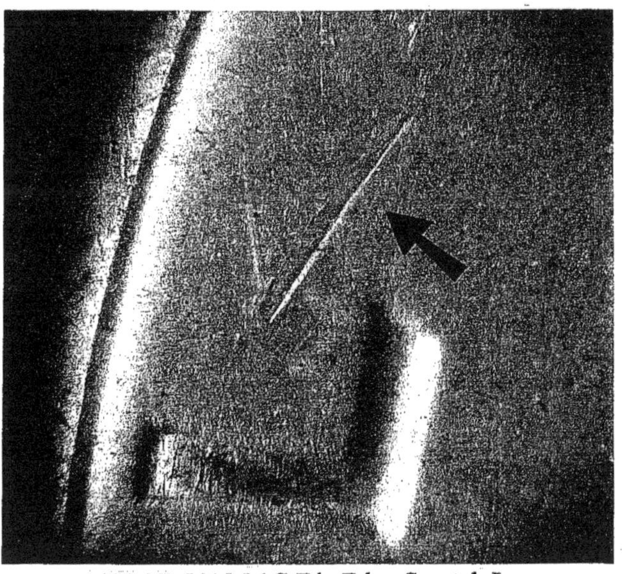
1926 D VAM 1C Die Edge Scratch L

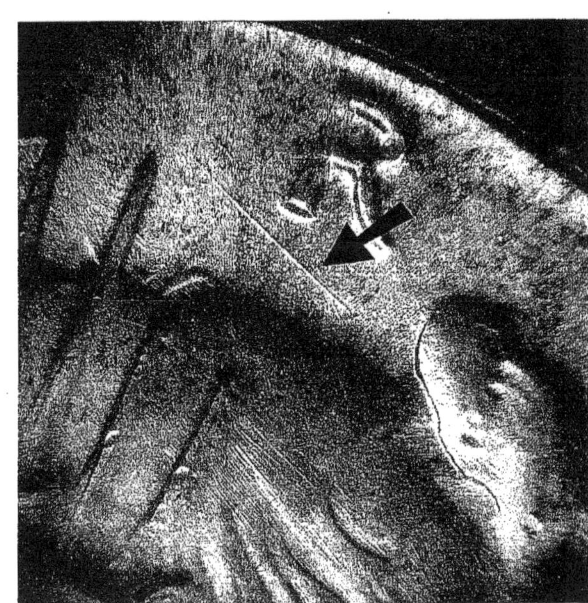
1926 S VAM 1N Die Edge Scratch R

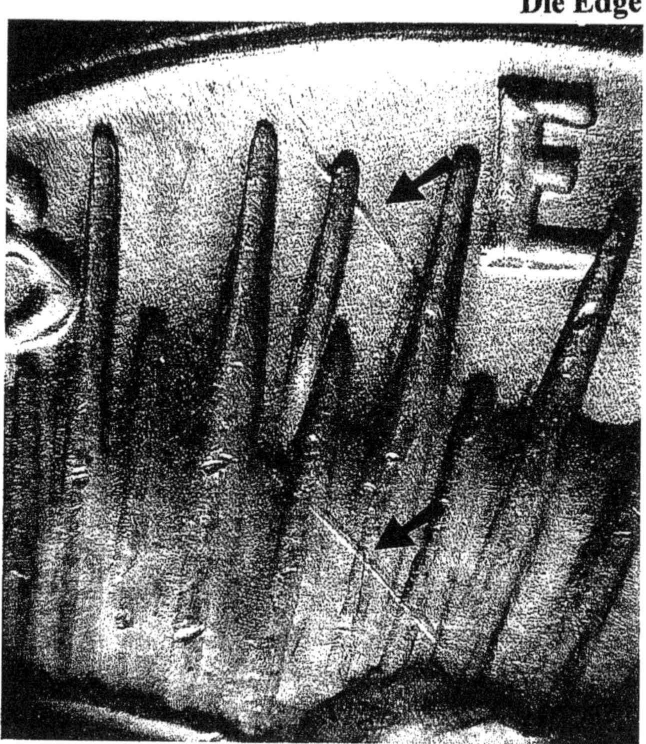

1927 D VAM 3A Die Edge Gouges E

APPENDIX C: Die Edge Gouges on Reverse

1922 P VAM 2AE Die Edge Gouge DOLL

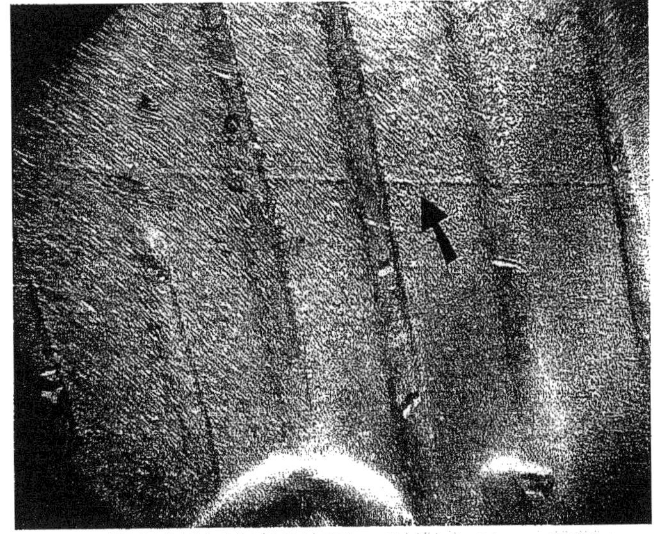
1922 P VAM 2BW Die Edge Scratch Above DOL

1922 D VAM 13B Die Edge Scratch Talon

1922 S VAM 1AD Die Edge Gouge A

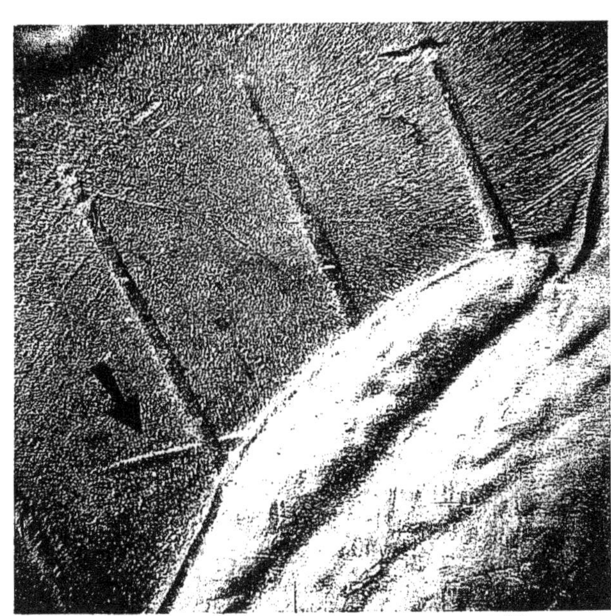
1922 S VAM 2M Die Edge Gouge Wing

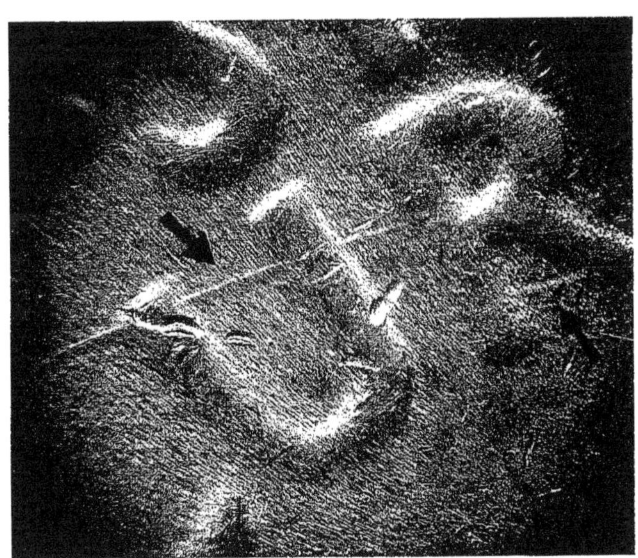
1922 S VAM 2AG1 Die Edge Gouges UR

1922 S VAM 2AB Die Edge Gouge Below AR

1923 P VAM 1AJ Die Edge Gouge Thru Ray

1923 D VAM 1G Die Edge Gouge Rays

1923 P VAM 1Q Die Edge Gouge in Rays Below Tail

1923 P VAM 1BI Die Edge Scratch TE

1923 S VAM 1BI Die Edge Scratch N

1925 P VAM 1P Die Edge Scratch Wing

1925 P VAM 17A Die Edge Gouge Above Hills

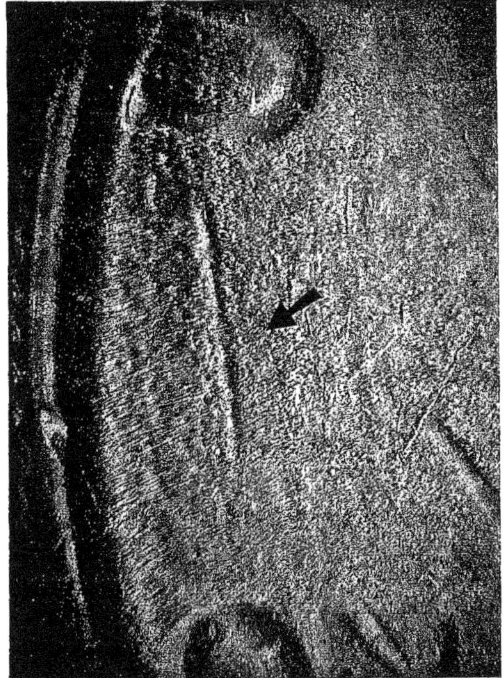

1925 S VAM 1C Die Edge Gouge Left of U

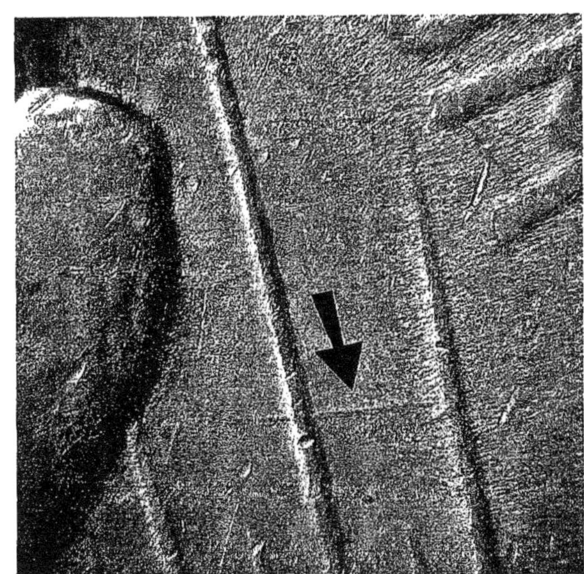

1935 P VAM 1A Die Edge Scratch Near Shoulder

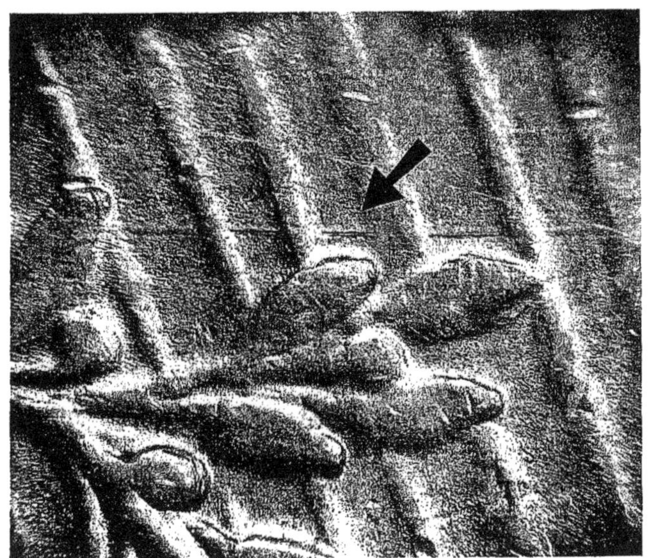

1935 P VAM 1A Die Edge Scratch Olive Leaves

1935 P VAM 1A Die Scratch R

1935 P VAM 1B Die Edge Scratch Rt Olive Leaves

1935 P VAM 1C Die Edge Scratch Across Ray

1935 S VAM 5A Die Edge Gouge Below Olive Leaves

APPENDIX D: Unexplained Die Gouges And Scratches

1921 Peace VAM 1B Die Gouge Above ONE

1921 Peace VAM 1K Oblong Die Gouge

1922 P VAM 1J Die Gouges Olive Branch

1922 P VAM 1M Die Scratch at 9

1922 P VAM 1S Die Scratch 1

1922 P VAM 2 O Die Gouge Below E

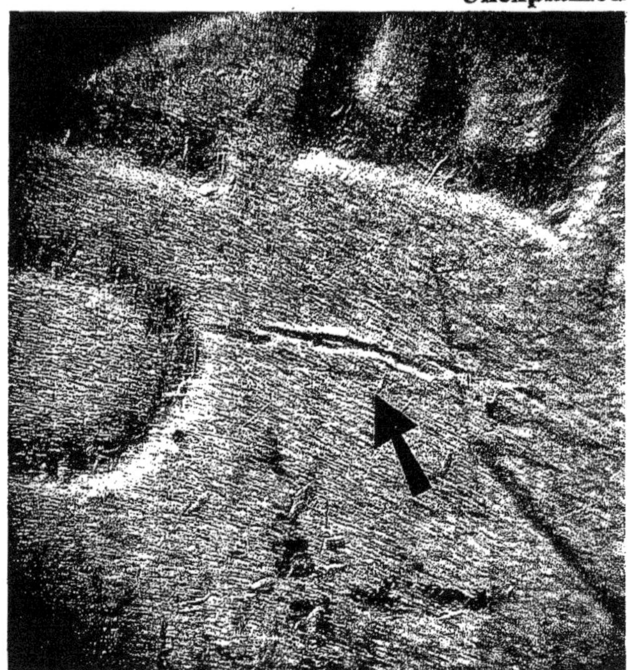

1922 P VAM 2P2 Die Scratch U

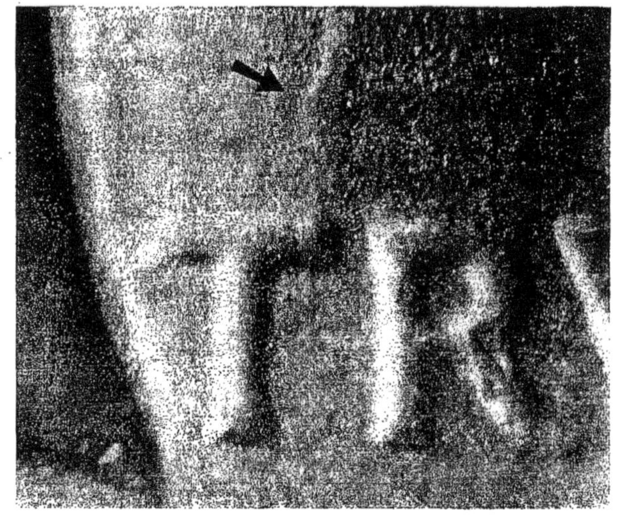

1922 P VAM 2Q Die Gouge Above T

1922 P VAM 2AD Tail on O

1922 P VAM 2AU Die Gouge T

1922 P VAM 2BM Die Gouge Olive Leaf

1922 P VAM 2BP Die Gouges UNITED

1922 P VAM 2BV Die Gouge O

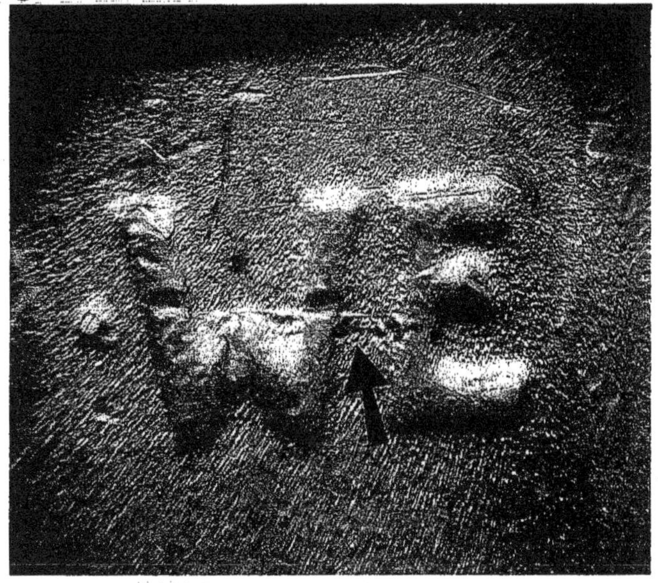

1922 P VAM 2CB Die Gouge WE

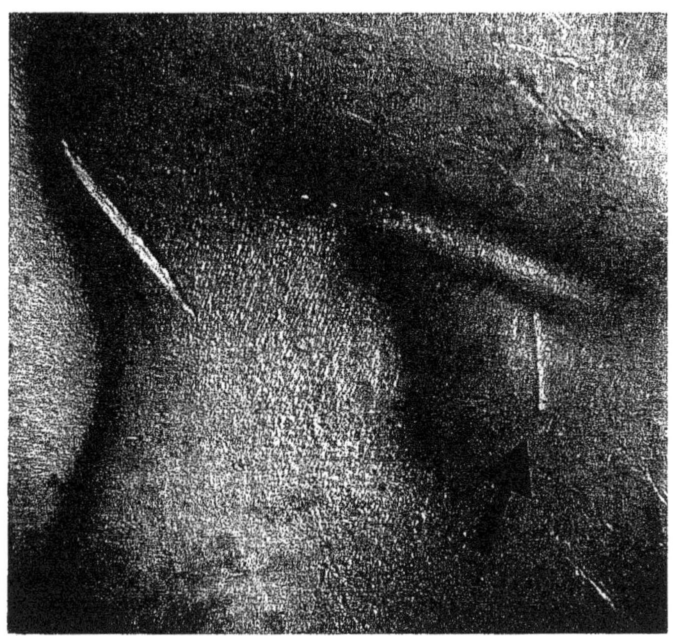

1922 P VAM 2CG Die Scratch Eye

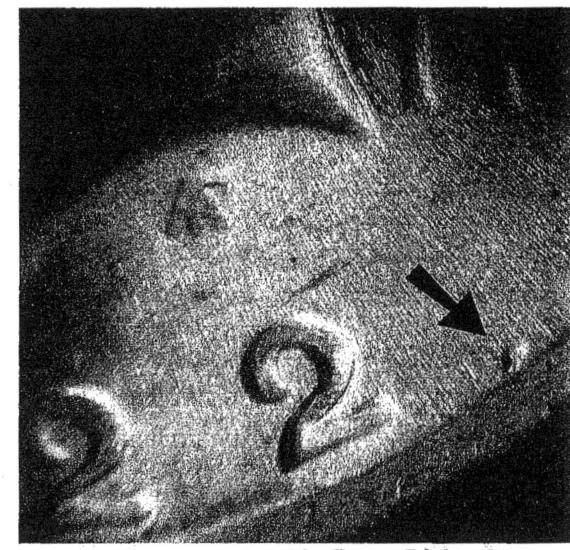

1922 P VAM 2CH Die Gouge Right of 2

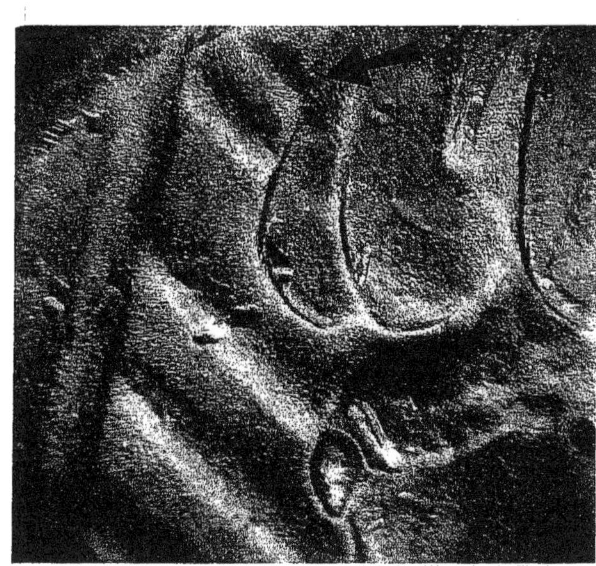

1922 P VAM 2CN Extra Ray Below Tail Feathers

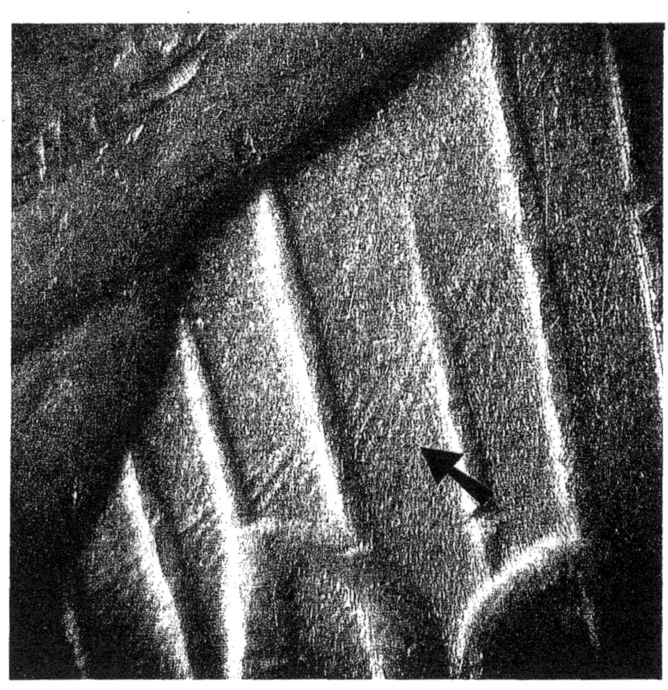

1922 P VAM 2DH Die Scratches Arc DO

Unexplained Die Gouges/Scratches

1922 P VAM 3 Die Gouge Forehead

1922 D VAM 8 Die Gouge B

1922 S VAM 2C Flaming Ray Die Gouge

1922 D VAM 1AA Die Gouge W, Die Scratch Chin

1922 S VAM 2A Spiked Tail Feather Die Gouge

1922 S VAM 2D Die Gouge G

1922 S VAM 2E Die Gouge Front Rays

1922 S VAM 2K Die Scratches B

1922 S VAM 2U Die Gouge Below WE

1923 P VAM 1I Die Gouge E

1923 P VAM 1T Die Gouge Lower Olive Leaves

1923 P VAM 1AC1 X Die Scratches

1923 P VAM 1AK Die Scratches NE

1923 P VAM 1BC Die Gouge Above Eagle's Neck

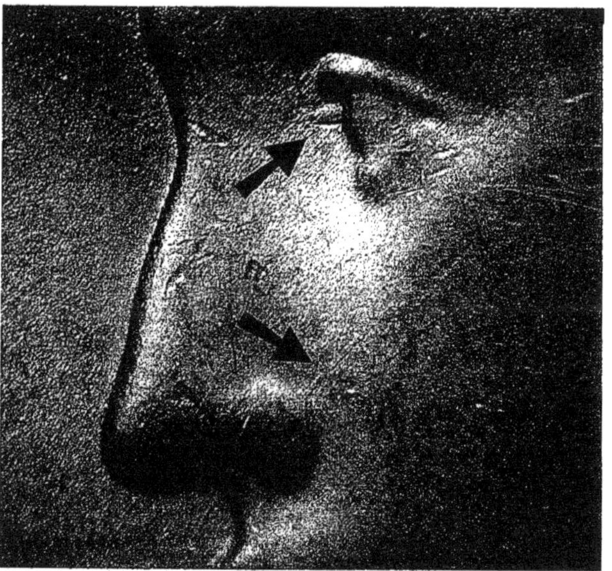

1923 P VAM 1BE Impaled Eye Die Scratch

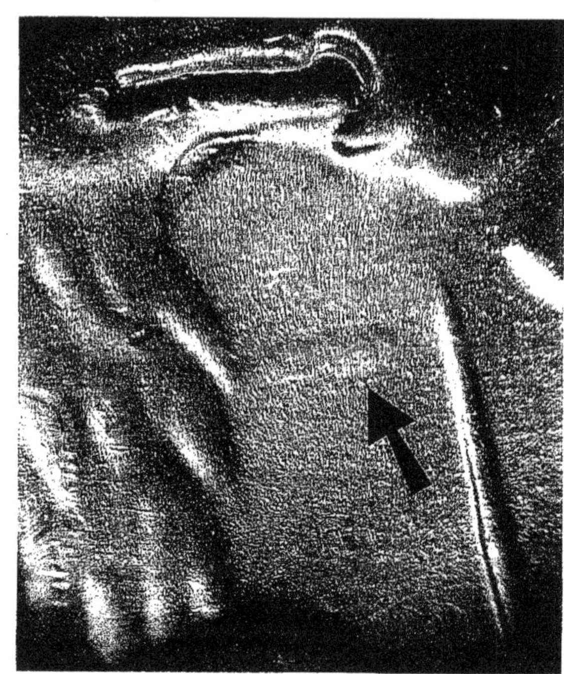

1923 P VAM 1BL Die Gouge Below Beak

1923 P VAM 1I Spiked Neck Die Gouge

1923 D VAM 1A Die Gouge Thru S

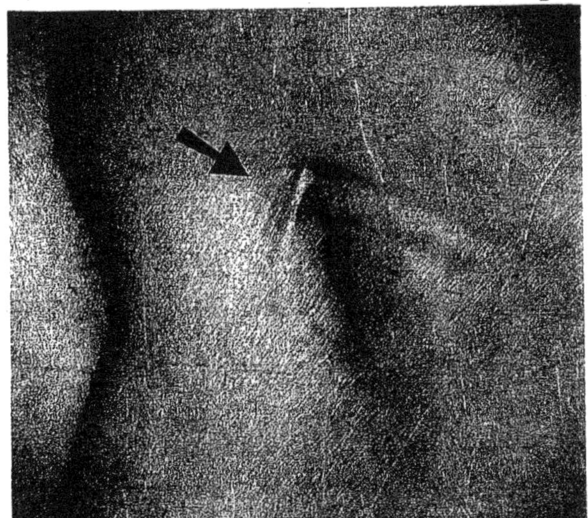

1923 D VAM 1AO1 Die Gouges Eye Front

1923 S VAM 1H Die Gouge 2

1923 S VAM 1V Die Gouge US

1923 S VAM 1AD3 Striated Die Scratch Above 2

1923 S VAM 1AQ1 Shallow Die Gouge B

1923 S VAM 1BK Die Scratch E

1924 P VAM 1J Thick Die Gouge Olive Leaves

1924 P VAM 1AP Die Scratches W

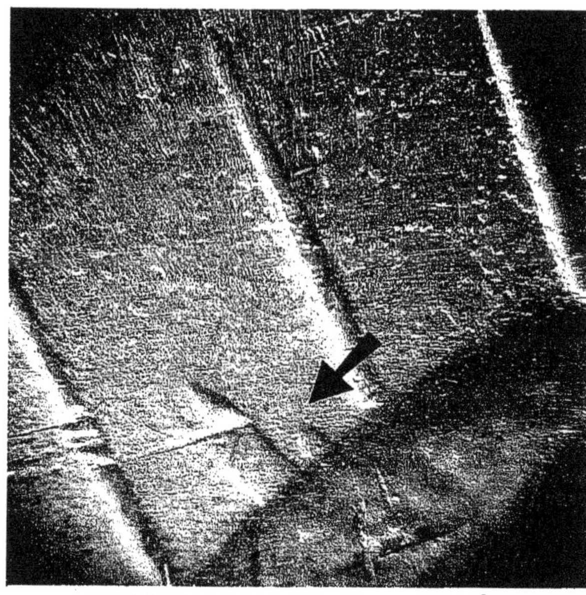
1924 P VAM 1AR Die Gouges & Pitting

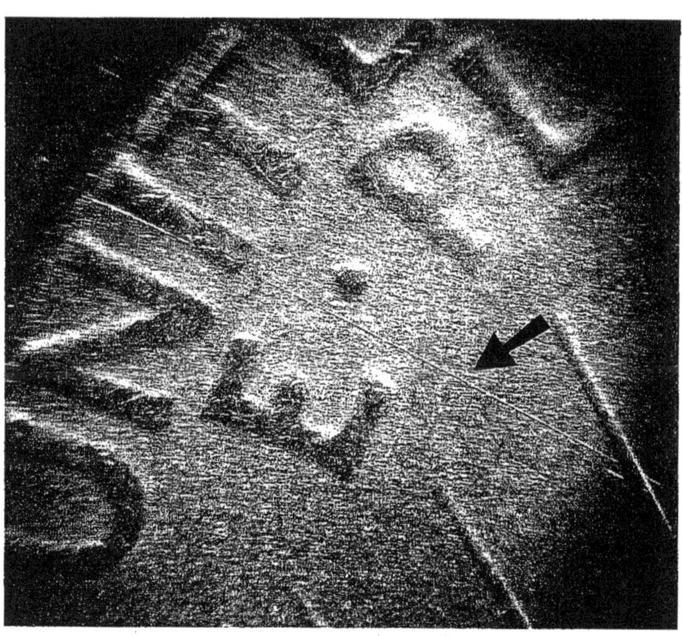
1924 S VAM 1H Long Die Scratch NI

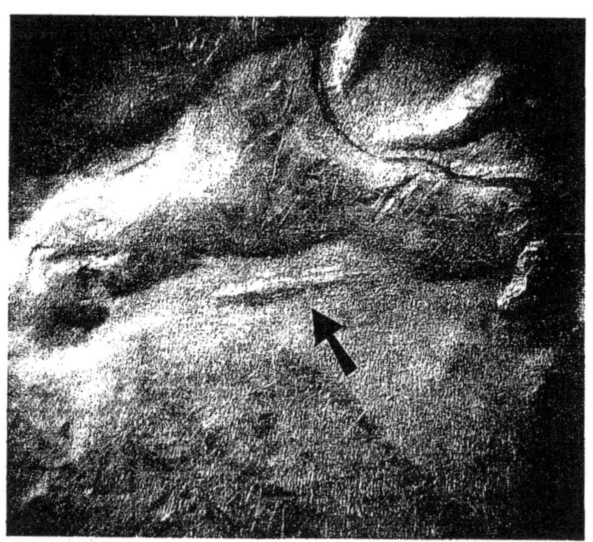
1924 S VAM 1J Die Gouge Eagle's Foot

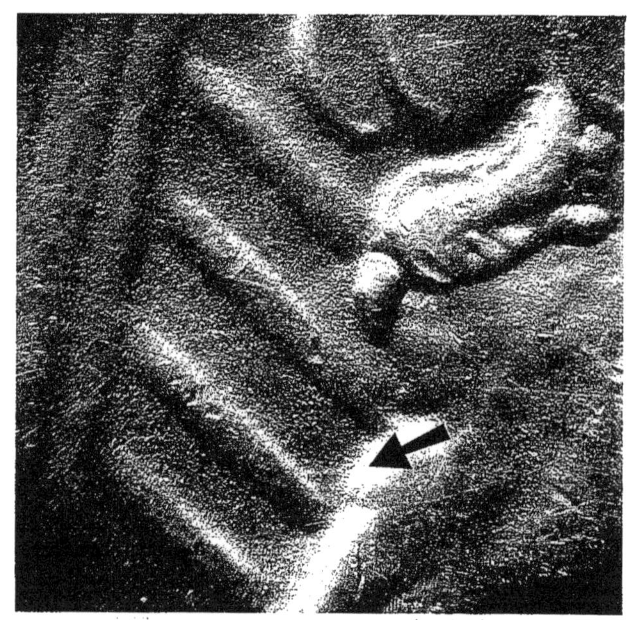
1924 S VAM 3 Die Scratch 3rd Ray

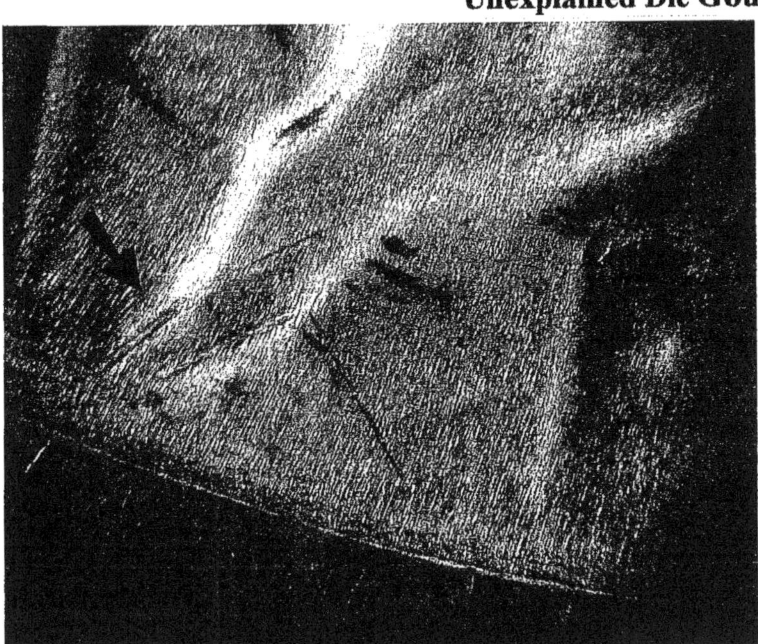
1925 P VAM 1AI Die Scratches Left of P

1925 S VAM 1F Die Gouge Below D

1926 S VAM 1Q Die Gouge B

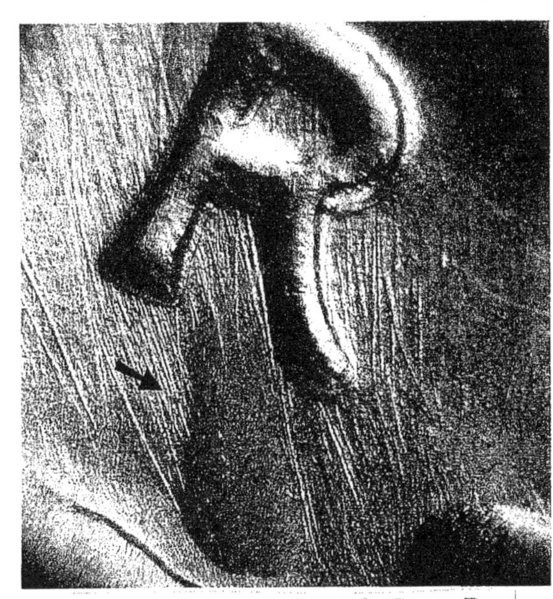
1926 S VAM 2A Comet Die Gouge R

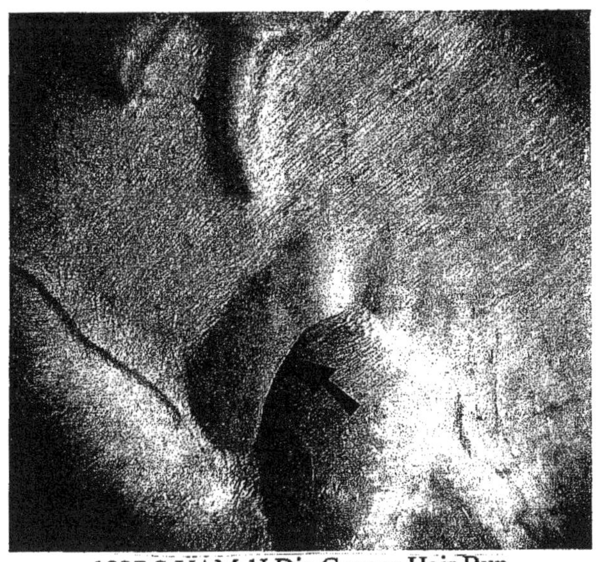
1927 S VAM 1I Die Gouges Hair Bun

1934 P VAM 1A Semi-circular Die Scratch

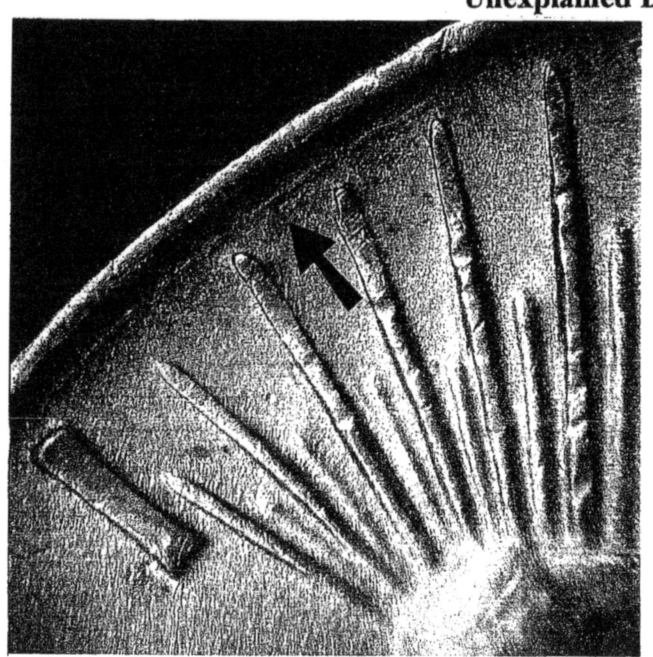

1934 P VAM 1D Die Gouge Rim at I

1934 P VAM 1F Die Gouge Lines in O

FURTHER REFERENCES

Please check Amazon Kindle for Michael S. Fey, Ph.D., and Leroy Van Allen & A. George Mallis publications. For hard copy print of books, please contact Dr. Fey at RCI, P.O. Box C, Ironia, NJ 07845 or eMail: Feyms@aol.com.

Hard copy books are also available at *The Institute for Silver Dollar Education and Research*, at website: *Ilovesilverdollars.org* or by contacting Executive Director John Baumgart at John.Baumgart@comcast.net

Amazon Kindle

Fey, Michael S. 2019. *The Complete Virtual Guide to Pricing Your Morgan Silver Dollars.* 286 pp. RCI

Van Allen, Leroy, & A. George Mallis. 2023. *Part I or II or III of Three. Comprehensive Catalog and Encyclopedia or Morgan & Peace Dollars.* RCI Total 520 pp.

Leroy Van Allen. 2011. *Wonders of Morgan Dollars*. 139 pp. RCI

Leroy Van Allen. 2013. *Wonders of Peace Dollars*. 273 pp. RCI

Leroy Van Allen. 2006. *Morgan Dollars 8 & 7 Over 8 Tail Feather Story*. 52 pp. RCI

Leroy Van Allen. 2010. *1878 P 7 Tail Feather Morgan Dollar Attribution Guide*. 130 pp. RCI

Leroy Van Allen. 2006. *1878 S Morgan Dollar Attribution Guide*. 139 pp. RCI

FURTHER REFERENCES

Hard Copy Books

Fey, Michael S. 2019. The Top 100 Morgan Dollar Varieties: The VAM Keys. 286 pp. RCI

Fey, Michael S. 2008. *A Decade of Top 100 Insights.* RCI 174 pp.

Van Allen, Leroy. 1991. *RotaFlip Die Rotation Booklet and Guide.* 1991. RCI

Kimpton, M.D., Mark. 2005. *Elite Clashed Morgan Dollars.* RCI 160 pp

Van Allen, Leroy, & A. George Mallis. 2023. *Comprehensive Catalog and Encyclopedia or Morgan & Peace Dollars.* RCI Total 520 pp.

Van Allen, Leroy 2011. *Wonders of Morgan Dollars.* 139 pp. RCI

Van Allen, Leroy 2013. *Wonders of Peace Dollars.* 273 pp. RCI

Van Allen, Leroy 2006. *Morgan Dollars 8 & 7 Over 8 Tail Feather Story.* 52 pp. RCI

Van Allen, Leroy 2010. *1878 P 7 Tail Feather Morgan Dollar Attribution Guide.* 130 pp. RCI

Van Allen, Leroy 2006. *1878 S Morgan Dollar Attribution Guide.* 139 pp. RCI

Van Allen, Leroy 2013. *Die Gouges and Scratches Peace Dollar Attribution Guide. 109 pp* RCI

Van Allen, Leroy 2008. *1921 Scribbles Morgan Dollar Attribution Guide.* 234 pp. RCI

Van Allen, Leroy. 2013. *Misplaced Date Digits Morgan Dollar Attribution Guide.* 57 pp RCI

Van Allen, Leroy. 2017. *Dashed Under 8 Morgan Dollar Attribution Guide.* 53 pp. RCI

Van Allen, Leroy. 2009. *Overdates and Over Mint Marks of Morgan Dollar Attribution Guide.* 53 pp. RCI

Van Allen, Leroy. 2015. *Denticle & Die Impressions Morgan Dollar Attribution Guide.* 109 pp. RCI

Van Allen, Leroy. 2009. *1921 P Infrequently Reeded or Wide Reeding Morgan Dollar Attribution Guide.* 31 pp. RCI

Van Allen, Leroy. 2011 *Amazing Changing 1921 S VAM 1B Thorn Head Morgan Dollar.* 2011. 22 pp. RCI

Van Allen, Leroy. 2009. *1889 P Doubled Ear Morgan Dollar Attribution Guide.* 32 pp. RCI

Van Allen, Leroy. 2016. *Micro o and Other Counterfeit Morgan and Peace Dollars.* 191 pp RCI

Van Allen, Leroy. 2005. *Micro o Mint Mark on Morgan Dollars.* 32 pp. RCI

Van Allen, Leroy. 2005. *Die Markers for 1921 Morgan and Peace Proof Dollars.* 9 pp. RCI

Van Allen, Leroy and Baumgart, John. 1992-Date Various VAM Book Yearly Supplements. RCI

www.ingramcontent.com/pod-product-compliance
Ingram Content Group UK Ltd.
Pitfield, Milton Keynes, MK11 3LW, UK
UKHW062000290726
14090UKWH00021B/1303

9 798991 964883